BOTH SIDES OF THE WATER
Essays on African-Native American Interactions

by Lonnie Harrington

PITTSBURGH, PENNSYLVANIA 15222

ISBN: 978-0-8059-9132-1
Library of Congress Control Number: 2005936295

Printed in the United States of America

First Printing

For information or to order additional books, please write:
RoseDog Books
701 Smithfield St.
Third Floor
Pittsburgh, PA 15222
U.S.A.
1-800-834-1803
Or visit our web site and
on-line bookstore at www.rosedogbookstore.com

TABLE OF CONTENTS

T hroughout oral and written history, people have interacted. This was (is) sometimes happening in positive situations, sometimes under the most adverse of circumstances. In the time period following 1492, various groups indigenous peoples of the western hemisphere and numerous African peoples found themselves caught up in events that still resound to this day. European countries such as Spain, Portugal, England, Holland, and France were to begin power struggles that were to sweep up the aforementioned peoples in its wake. The results of this were devastating. The exploitation of people, land and her resources was to be the legacy of the establishing of the Americas. Africans and indigenous peoples of the western hemisphere were to suffer the horrors of slavery (although the trade in humans was to shift numerically toward Africans as time progressed). With this backdrop, Africans and native peoples began to interact under crises conditions. To deal with these conditions, alliances formed all over the hemisphere. These peoples often came to the aid of each other, and in some instances, inter-married and integrated into settings best described as communities.

This meant that some victims of enslavement found sanctuary and assimilated into already established settings and, in other instances, new communities would form. This in turn led the colonizing Europeans to devise a broad spectrum of divide and conquer tactics, tactics that have lasted into contemporary times. One of the worst fears of the colonies was the threat of black-red alliances opposing their efforts on any number of fronts. These fears certainly were justified in varying degrees, and it was a reality that was to be played out time and time again over the centuries as the victims of European expansion fought back. The history of these interactions, as well as interactions created by other sets of circumstances, live on in family legacies.

What does it mean to acknowledge and retain an identity of multiple racial ancestry in a situation where the dominant social structure has for centuries influenced attitudes by dictating and enforcing monolithic racial identification? Divide and conquer tactics have been and remain relentless. As the twenty first century progresses, the tactics are not necessarily as overt, such as sending military forces against communities (although at times, the threat is a continued reality, as in reports of Operation Gallant Piper in New York State in the mid 1990s). Contemporary strategies take the form of legislative assaults, something that started during Europe's colonization of the hemisphere and has continued to refine itself. If one believes in a level playing field, it becomes apparent that dominant institutions continue to use multiple ancestry as a tool to its advantage while racial groups and multiethnic peoples are subjected to negative situations. Some victimized communities have adopted some of the dominant culture's attitudes, out of a perceived sense of survival. The dominant culture attempts to force individuals to choose one side of one's ancestry over the other. Within communities often to acknowledge another aspect of one's heritage beyond lip service is to run the risk of ridicule. Dominating social attitudes reinforce and strengthen stereotypes because it is for the most part politically convenient and advantageous. This has often been an obstacle for building connections based on commonalities. But the reality runs head-on with these attitudes in a place like the western hemisphere where many racial, ethnic, religious, and nationality groups have interacted for centuries. While interaction is certainly not a new phenomenon, in the Americas, groups from all over the globe have relocated into areas where descendants of the original inhabitants continue to maintain a presence, one that is ignored when it's convenient to do so, but a presence none the less.

It has been argued in some circles that the policies of the European entities that invaded the western hemisphere were substantially different in their approach. Spain and France to whatever degree implemented assimilation strategies. The English moved in the direction of eradication. All were implemented with varying degrees of brutality and deceit. What kind of social/political atmosphere was created as a result of the hemispheric invasion, as opposed to the conditions that existed prior to this upheaval? What are the results that have taken place in the years of increased contacts between various groups of people who have interacted in an atmosphere of crises for much of this period (since 1492). One common denominator is blood. The native peoples of the western hemisphere and the sons and daughters of Africa share bloodlines. There is a large indigenous presence in African American communities, and many families across the United States make mention of having Indians in the family tree. In some reservation communities, there are Native Americans that share African ancestry. Yet in the minds of some, an individual who has African ancestry and maintains a sense of identity as also being native to the western hemisphere is still at best difficult to comprehend and/or acknowledge, much less accept. This occurs frequently, and I dare say commonly, as there are those find it absurd that anyone can have mixed African-Native bloodlines and be "Indian". To some in the native community who have remained culturally conservative (traditional), there is no prefix necessary (as in the term "Black Indian"). You either are or you are not, regardless of blood quantum.

Blood quantum is an explosive topic, especially as this criteria has been imposed to the degree of dictating attitudes as to who is and who isn't "Indian". Without a doubt (in the United States) those who are enrolled members of a "Recognized" tribe or nation are eligible for services that are suppose to be obligated by treaty. The CDIB (Certificate of Degree of Indian Blood) card has become a goal for some individuals who desire to prove for any number of reasons that at least by government standards they are "Indian". And while many recognized tribal governments are responsible for making this determination, this is a survival response to criteria set down primarily by federal entities. Whereas, historically indigenous communities would have their citizenry comprised of those who were not only born of the specific people (as far as bloodlines were concerned), but those who had been adopted or intermarried into a family or clan within the community. Prior to the encounter of October 12, 1492, this meant that many indigenous communities were already multi faceted as far as who were members of that specific community. This is because intermarriage and adoption was hardly a new concept. The response to outside pressures that determine who is and who isn't is a form of undermining sovereignty. Similar to what has occurred in parts of the world historically (Apartheid South Africa, Nazi Germany, and the United States until the 1960s), these circumstances set up scenarios for extinction by paper (and other means). In August of 2001, the Bureau of Indian Affairs (BIA) of the U.S. Department of the Interior, announced that there were to be forums held among tribal representatives to discuss new standards of examining blood quantums that were proposed to be implemented. And while leaders in recognized communities realized the importance of establishing set criteria for establishing who may be eligible for membership in their respective communities, many also saw this as another threat to the sovereignty of their nations, as many rightly believe that only they should determine who is welcome among them. The fact is that some native nations and communities were and are multi racial. That is, the make up of the people are such due to the fact of intermarriage and or adoption. And some have fought and won the right to be recognized as indigenous. There are at least two notable examples of communities of mixed ancestry winning the right to be (in governmental eyes) native. The *Metis* of Canada and the *Garifuna of Central America* and the Caribbean are two prominent examples.

The Metis are descendants of Cree People who intermarried with French and Scots. During the colonial period French men as well as other European men wanted a share of the fur trade. As a result, white men traveled into the interior lakes, rivers and forests to seek out those animals whose fur was a marketable commodity. Beaver was especially prized, but not to the exclusion of other animals. This meant that these travelers would inevitably have contacts with the native peoples of the areas they journeyed. In some instances, these men married native women. Over time the descendants of these unions would establish a unique culture. By the 1880s communities of Meti were prominent in parts of western Canada, as well as northern Montana. Their lifestyle was semi sedentary, as many farmed part of the year living in dwellings similar to their white counterparts, and at other times of the year, organized into units to hunt buffalo.

During this period many would live in tepees. There were to be three major confrontation with the Canadian Government in succession, increasing in their intensity. These were the Courthouse Rebellion of 1849 and the First and Second Riel's Rebellions of 1869 and 1885. Although the Meti won the right for border access for commerce (1849),and the establishment of a recognized homeland (1869), treaty violations were to lead to the 1885 confrontation, which was more violent. The Meti were to ally with some of their Cree relations in this third encounter. In the end, the Meti and Cree would succumb to the militarily superior numbers of the Canadians. Yet they would be recognized as an indigenous people. The Garifuna are descendant of Carib people who intermarried with Africans. There is some evidence that suggests the interaction between Africans and Caribs pre date 1492. After the hemispheric invasion began, Africans would escape to remote parts of islands occupied by Caribs, such as Dominica, Grenada, the Virgin Islands, and Saint Vincent. There was some intermarriage between the groups of people. Over time, European powers would come to recognize distinct Carib communities, red and black. There were periods of (an uneasy) peace as well as war. After the last uprising on Saint Vincent occurred in 1795, the stage was set. As European domination gained footholds throughout the Caribbean, many Caribs were deported (although some managed to remain on the islands of Saint Vincent and Dominica). Some were to end up on the island of Roatan, located off of Honduras. Others would end up in Honduras and Belize. Today groups of people recognizing themselves as Carib are found on Dominica, Trinidad, and Saint Vincent, as well as those individuals of this ancestry who live in other parts of the world. Garifuna communities are readily identified in Honduras, Nicaragua, and Belize. While many members of these communities have African features, there is the legacy of language retention, specifically Carib, that exists in varying degrees found in these areas. As a result of diasporic activities, there are now sizable Garifuna populations in the United States.

In the highly racialized environment of the western hemisphere however, concepts and ideologies with a strong prejudicial bias based on perceptions of race have continued to impact people across the spectrum of ethnicity. This often flies in the face of the fact that for centuries there have been those who have maintain indigenous cultural retention (of whatever degree) and indeed shared these bloodlines. This has been done and continues to be so within the geographic confines of reservation communities, as well as in urban and rural settings where people have banded together, sometimes as community organizations, sometimes in less formal (but no less important) settings. These groups are not necessarily tribal entities, but provide support in an atmosphere that remains negative, at times to the point of hostility. Racial animosity is still a fact of life in the Americas. And whereas people of mixed descent are a factor, the history of interaction also shows that divide and conquer strategies played havoc wherever and however they were implemented. In the late twentieth century and at the beginning of the twenty-first, there has been an increase in the number of forums that examine this phenomenon. Yet for some individuals who use the term "Black Indian" for whatever reason (that is one of African and native ancestry relating to and/or retaining cultural protocols) outside of family and some limited academic circles, more often than not, continue to draw reactions of disbelief and ridicule (at the very least). History can be ignored; it can be manipulated. It is said with justification that history is written from the standpoint of the conqueror(s). Despite this fact, it is reality that testifies to the truth of the matter. In this work, I have not set out to glorify, nor demonize. It is necessary to examine the good and the bad that form the whole picture. I feel it is time that we, meaning those of us who have these backgrounds and cultural perspectives tell our own stories. There have been and will continue to be outsiders, some sincere, others with whatever agenda, who seek to present their points of view. Mine certainly is not the only version of what has happened and is happening. This is not a comprehensive work. I doubt if such a work can actually be accomplished in one, two, or whatever number of volumes. As I haved compiled these essays over a number of years, certain events mentioned in this work continue to evolve.

In the time I worked on this project I felt it was important to look at a number of scenarios and place them into context as to be able to have an objective perspective. This means numerous issues are approached. There are commonalties of experiences, for there are a large number of people of mixed ancestry who observe cultural protocols as part of lifestyle. There are also situations that many people of color, and especially economically disenfranchised people, find themselves facing that again are a common phenomenon. With all of this as background material as well as my own life experiences, this work is no doubt coming from my point of view.

"Both continents, Africa and America, be it remembered, were "discovered" - what a wealth of arrogance that little word contains! - with devastating results for the indigenous populations, whose only human use thereafter was a source of capital for white people. On both continents the white and dark gods met in combat, and it is on the outcome of this combat that the future of both continents depends."

From "No Name In The Street", c.1972 by James Baldwin. Copyright renewed. Reprinted by arrangement with the James Baldwin Estate

Three had been a time when the very mention of pre Columbian contacts between people of Turtle Island and Africa would be dismissed as impossible and be subject to the very least with ridicule. Professionals in academic settings that were involved in research around this topic found it difficult to have any type of rational discourse. With the increased exposure of various types of evidence in the western hemisphere as well as Africa of artifacts and items found and dated long before European intervention, increased discussions are taking place to seriously examine these phenomenon.

Taino Tee! (Taino)
Aleecooba! (Arawak)
En-Yah-Tah-Fay! (Mali)
Kay Mee Say Rahkee! (Aymara)

The above are greetings. Three are of the western hemisphere; one is from Africa. Was this the way that early African travelers and native peoples of Turtle Island and the Caribbean greeted each other? Perhaps we will never know the specifics of the first encounter. So much has been lost because of the suppression of information (both oral, and, contrary to some academic perspectives, written) that the exact time and place will more than likely never be known. If the wide body of evidence is examined it can be surmised that some of the earliest contacts occurred between 1200 to 900 BC. Through the research of individuals in academic circles such as Professor Ivan Van Sertimer, Leo Weiner, and the late Professor Barry Fell (among others), there is a large body of work that is available that documents contacts that existed between representatives of two hemispheres which encompass Africa and what is now called North and Central America during this aforementioned timeframe. More than likely, early travelers arriving at points on the east Atlantic seacoasts, be they from Africa or Europe reached these destinations by accident. As we look at the body of information we find that mariners found themselves in ocean currents that at the time would have been extremely difficult to negotiate, given the existing marine technology of the day. The terminus points of these currents would have enabled sailors to make landfall at numerous locations throughout this hemisphere. It is in places such as the ancient Olmec Empire that we have one example of evidence testifying to these contacts. Artists of this empire were indeed gifted and have left their legacy by many works, some of which include statues. Fourteen of many "Olmec Heads" stand in massive, dignified testimony to these sets of circumstances. Artists of this civilization captured images in boulders of basalt. Some of these statues weigh in at an impressive twenty tons. These images are of Africans. Researchers have stated that the facial features and headdresses illustrated on these works in particular resemble what some soldiers of the time period looked like. The period that is referred to here covers the time frame of 200 to 700 B.C.. What was happening on the land masses we now call Africa and the Americas at the point in time of early contacts?

What kind of activities would lead to the encounters of peoples who covered geographic distances measuring thousands of miles? What impact would social/political pressures play (and continue to play) in the chapters of stories to be told? In the areas now called Central and South America, societies were building great urban centers, along with the support systems needed to maintain this way of life. The foundations established in this part of the world would serve as the basis for many other civilizations that followed over the course of centuries. It is during the time period of 1500 to 600 B.C. that the Olmec Civilization (People of the Jaguar) rose to the forefront of the world that was known to them. Located in the region on the southern coast of the Gulf of Mexico, urban centers were established such as Tres Zapotes, San Lorenzo, and La Venta (in contemporary terminology). A network of rural areas linked these cities with resources to survive. The surrounding country side was rich in environmental resources crucial to any kind of settlement, large or small, urban or rural. With abundant food supplies coming from nature as well as organized agricultural efforts that had for centuries produced beans, chilis, tomatoes, squash, and maize (among other crops), Olmec society came onto its own. Similar development patterns are observed with other civilizations such as the Zapotec (500 B.C. to A.D.700) who had some interaction with Olmecs and shared similar traits such as the characteristic mounds, and if we look northward for examples, we find the Hopewell and Mississippian Cultures which came into prominence around 100 B.C. to A.D.400 and A.D.750 to A.D.1539 respectively. The cultures located in what is now called North America were pre dated by the Adena Culture of the Ohio River Valley region (8000 B.C. to 1000 B.C.), which also had engaged in mound construction. Adena and Hopewell societies engaged in limited agriculture, as the environmental resources available were rich in their offerings. The Mississippian civilization shared traits of the great civilizations located in what has been designated as Meso America. As late as A.D.1500 the Natchez of the southeast resembled social structures that could have easily been identified in many ways as Mexica (Aztec). Indeed similarities between social systems can be seen also around the Caribbean Basin area now called the Gulf of Mexico as Arawak, Mississippian, Mayan and Mexica interacted. Names such as Olmec, Toltec, Mayan, and Mexica would have an impact on world history.

During these times, Arawakan peoples had begun their slow and steady progress of migration from areas of Central and Northern South America into the islands of the Antilles. As these migrants settled, their new homeland(s) would be called Borinken, Quisqueya, Yahmayca,and Guanahani, among others. What is still a topic of debate among some Taino scholars is that on an island close to what is now called Florida, these migrants came in touch with the Ciboney (Guanahatabeys), and eventually integrated these people into their culture. This happened on the island called Cuba. It would be from these various islands that had established societies, commercial and social endeavors with each other and the lands north and west would occur. They were also to receive travelers from these ares as well as from across the Atlantic Ocean. In the islands now called the Bahamas, the Lucayo would be the first of the hemisphere to experience the beginning of the hemispheric invasion (although there had been prior contacts in the hemisphere over centuries that were not qualified to be termed invasive). Words and terms now common in the United States can be traced directly to the Tainos of the Caribbean: canoe, barbecue, tobacco, hurricane, etc. The Tainos (as some debate) were to be followed into the Antilles and at times come in conflict with others who also would migrate into the islands. It is from this group of people, the Caribs, that these islands, the surrounding waters, and parts of the continental land masses that bordered this area would be classified and known. By the time of the hemispheric invasion that began in 1492, a vast trade network existed, spanning throughout the land masses of the hemisphere and the islands of the Caribbean. Traders carried on their endeavors by foot and/or by watercraft of varying sizes. On many of the riverways, small canoes served the task at hand.

In the Gulf of Mexico and off the southeastern coast of what is now the United States, larger vessels capable of carrying up to thirty or forty people traveled over the water routes between the mainland and the islands. This covered an area that included the islands of the Caribbean, the basin of the Gulf of Mexico, and the west coast of Florida. In Africa, Egypt was still in its glory, although there was a constant ebb and flow of upheavals brought on from within the culture as well as from outside invaders. On the coast of North Africa, Carthage, the society that gave rise to the military daring and genius of Hannibal, had to deal with its situations, and their armies would continue to command respect over a wide region. During this time, its maritime fleets ranged not only into the Mediterranean Sea and the Red Sea, but along the coast of West Africa. During the dynasties of Egypt, maritime vessels ranged primarily eastward, but from time to time would venture westward, thus bringing themselves into the range of the currents that extended from Africa to points in the Caribbean and off Central and South America. Looking at the locations of some of the urban centers of the Olmec civilization, we can see that some of these terminus points were in close proximity. It was in these currents that the first African vessel(s) were caught by surprise and found themselves being taken to points west, ultimately ending up in the Caribbean,and Central and South America. Some scholars believe it was during the reign of the Egyptian King Rameses III that the first contacts between Turtle Island and Africa took place around 1200 B.C. During the reign of Necho II of Egypt (circa 600 B.C.) seacraft were sailing the waters of coastal Africa in all directions in compliance with royal orders. The crews of these vessels were multi ethnic, comprised of Nubians, Phoenicians, and Egyptians of varying blood-lines. Thor Heyerdahl was to prove during the 1960s that an "African" designed seacraft was capable of making a transatlantic voyage. He would travel from Africa to South America in a seacraft of ancient African design and construct, thus giving credence to the possibility of transoceanic travel by African mariners.

The United States Government has acknowledged the possibility of pre-columbian contacts between Africans and indigenous peoples of what is now North America. In the 1894 United States Department of the Interior Census of the Five Civilized Tribes, when surveying the subgroups of the Creek Confederacy that had been forcibly relocated to Oklahoma, it was acknowledged under the Yamasee: "Believed to be descendent of shipwrecked African sailors and Indian women". Abubakari of Mali was one African ruler who decided to undertake the endeavor of finding out what was beyond the western horizon. The first expedition that he sponsored left the west coast of Mali in approximately 1309. One ship that returned reported that the other ships of the expedition had been caught in a "river in the ocean". This captain decided to turn back rather than risk his crew. As a result of this report, Abubakari led the second expedition, making one of his landings in what is now southern Mexico in approximately A.D.1310-11. It would be Abubakari's half brother that came into renown for his epic journey to and from Mecca in 1323-4, this being Mansa Musa. It must be noted that Christopher Columbus did not set out to sail west directly from Spain. The vessels under his command first headed south to the west coast of Africa. His brother Bartalomew, who would accompany him on later voyages, had been a mapmaker in the court of Dom Joao 11 of Portugal. Bartalomew Columbus had reports from his contacts who had traveled along west Africa that for years African seacraft had been seen headed due west sailing past the Cape Verde and Canary Islands with full loads of cargo. After the 1492 contact and subsequent invasion of the western hemisphere which commenced as a result of Columbus's initial voyage, native men (and to a lesser extent women) of what was to become known as the Americas who fell victim to European slaving expeditions would end up (as one destination) on these islands.

Those Europeans who returned from the western hemisphere found out many things. Among the things was evidence of contacts between other civiliza-tions with the native cultures of the hemisphere. The many societies of Turtle Island were as diverse as any other part of the world. There were all degrees of governing structures, ranging from the simple to complex. There were numerous rural cultures. There were loose, autonomous bands. There were all degrees of confederations. There were sophisticated urban cultures that rivaled and in instances surpassed what was existing in Europe at the time. Indeed some the urban centers had fallen; others rose as replacement.

There had already been the glory of the culture of Chaco Canyon in the southwest (in what is now New Mexico). Cahokia, a large urban center near the junction of the Mississippi and Missouri Rivers at its peak was about the size of Manhattan (New York City). Its residents numbered well into the thousands. Part of this legacy was left with the numerous Mound cultures of the midwest and east that were magnificent in their own right, although smaller. The Spanish conquistador Cortez and entourage marveled at the site of Tenotchitlan, where Mexico City now stands. Yet the phenomenon of intercontinental contact was not restricted in terms of direction east to west. As early as 60 B.C., there were reports in central coastal Europe that there were marooned mariners who had been stranded because their maritime craft had been taken off course by bad weather conditions. These men are described by latter historians as "Indians". While there may be the inclination to think of Asians, one only needs to look at which body of water is   prevalent on the western coastal regions of Europe; this being the Atlantic Ocean. These shipwrecked mariners could have been the ancestors of some contemporary Algonquin, Muskogean, Souixan, or another group of people (of what is now the eastern United States) known in these times. While there has been in recent times various forums that have taken place to discuss and examine the nature of interaction in this hemisphere, one may (and should) also ask, what happened to those victims who were kidnapped and shipped eastward? To those kidnapped natives of the western hemisphere who found themselves being enslaved in North Africa?, West Africa? the Cape Verde Islands? As fate would have it some Cape Verdeans have migrated to New England, a place where some of the earliest victims in this story began to be subjected to the trauma in the wake of expanding European interests. One can speculate it is quite possible that some of these Cape Verdeans carry in their bodies the bloodlines of some of the indigenous people from the western hemisphere.

When examining events in Africa after the Berlin Conference of 1884-5, the sad parallels can be compared. Indigenous peoples at various points on the Earth had suffered in the face of the tide of imperialism at the hands of numerous European governments. In what is now the United States, the legacy that began with the English, French, and Spanish (predominately), was now being carried on by their descendants who called themselves Americans. Pain and sadness left its own pathetic trail. Africa, which had already seen atrocities via the slave trade and had borne intrusions on its lands, now felt the full might of colonizing entities that seemed willing to stop at nothing to further plunder this area of the Earth. Sand Creek Wyoming, in November 1864, Black Kettle's Band of Cheyenne with some Arapaho allies attacked at dawn by Colorado militia commanded by John Chivington. The Great Swamp Massacre in Rhode Island, in December 1675, where more than 1000 colonists from Plymouth attack a Narragansett village, torching the town of the Sachem Canochet.

Pound Ridge, Westchester County New York in March 1644, where a contingent of Dutch under the command of the English mercenary John Underhill, attacked and torched a village of Wappinger people. These scenarios which also have parallels in Central and South America, as well as the Caribbean, are examples of barbaric acts focused on indigenous people, and now are to have their equals throughout Africa. And while this was nothing new to Africa, it was to escalate to heights that are best characterized as aberrations. What had started with the slave trade now perversely multiplied as the body counts began to rise. Algeria, Egypt, Ethiopia, Ghana, Sudan, Angola, Belgian Congo, Kenya,

Dahomey, Nigeria, Uganda, Cameroon, Togo, Namibia, and Tanzania, are just a few locales that were to bear witness to atrocities committed in the name of colonial expansion by England, Portugal, Germany, Belgium, France, and Italy. As in other parts of the world, the colonizers would use native warriors to fight other native peoples. This is a pattern that has a frightening ring of deja vu. At the beginning of the twenty-first century Africa has managed to shake itself loose of the physical presence of many colonizing entities, although economic predation and resource exploitation is still a fact. By and large throughout the Americas it is the descendants of the post 1492 colonizers who are still calling the shots.

The fact is that kidnapped Africans (and free blacks that decided to take their chances elsewhere) who were being assimilated into native communities as participating members were a direct threat to the interests of the colonizers everywhere in the hemisphere. It would be a mistake to presume that social conditions were utopian. Yet the social climate among native cultures of this hemisphere offered alternative lifestyles that were more dignified than roles faced by persons of color in the slaveholding European societies that was expanding in the Americas. All societies have their strengths and shortcomings. But these examples of social equity were not to be tolerated. The results of divide and conquer tactics, sometimes subtle and implemented in varying degrees of sophistication are still present in contemporary times.

Commonality, Diversity, Adversity

Slavery. If ever there was a situation that could be linked to the concept of perverse economic stimulus and the height of moral degradation, it's slavery, and certainly, the Trans-Atlantic Slave Trade serves as one tragic example. The very word brings up images and thoughts that are totally repulsive. For many people of color, and for that matter people of European ancestry, this is a topic of which the effects are still being felt today at the beginning of the twenty-first century. Racism and classism has had a dramatic impact on the soul of people of this hemisphere. Many attitudes that are prevalent today can be traced directly to the Trans-Atlantic Slave Trade, and the multitude of rationales that tried to morally justify this atrocity. There is no doubt that forms of slavery have existed on all parts of the Earth. Africa and Turtle Island are no exception. Yet if we closely look at what was considered slavery prior to 1492, we must analyze the circumstances that we are examining objectively. I will state firmly that in my opinion, the idea of slavery in any form is an abomination.

In what became the United States, the phenomenon of slavery certainly existed. Before the importation of kidnapped Africans began to reach its obscene heights, the indigenous people of this part of the world found themselves fulfilling the role of being enslaved. Thus, as the most precious resource of Africa, her sons and daughters of the land were kidnapped and shipped over the Atlantic Ocean, they were fed into a pre-existing system of slavery and as time passed, this system became more horribly refined. As fate would have it, history repeated itself during the nineteenth and twentieth centuries in Africa as the land itself was divided up and exploited by various European countries, especially after the Berlin Conference of 1884-5. By this point in time, many of these European countries had centuries of experience in exploiting the Americas and other lands and their respective indigenous populations. In contemporary times, the actions of entities such as the World Bank and the International Monetary Fund have been critiqued by some that champion social justice as a more contemporary manifestation of the Berlin Conference. It seems that economic predation against numerous indigenous communities worldwide over the centuries has taken on a different guise and continues to be the rule as opposed to the exception.

In the case of the area now called the Americas, some of its native inhabitants were enslaved while the land base was taken away, to shrink time and time again. In Africa too, its people would be enslaved, although many were to suffer the fate of being transported to lands across the Atlantic Ocean. Similar to what was happening in the Americas, many African countries found themselves unknowingly becoming consumers in a global economy. The dependence on European goods infiltrated African and Turtle Island societies and, to an extent, undermined self-reliance on both sides of the Atlantic Ocean. Eurocentric-oriented Christianity, which ironically had its roots in the cultures of dark-skinned peoples, assaulted traditional spiritual belief systems. While some of these European countries had gained footholds on coastal regions around Africa, the onslaught to steal the land itself was not to shift into high gear until the mid 1880s. Many cultures native to Turtle Island indulged in forms of slavery. Raids with the goal of enslavement was nothing new on either side of the ocean. References are found throughout the histories (oral and written) of many people. Often war captives found themselves in the position of becoming slaves for the conquerors. This theme has been repeated throughout the world over the millennium. What must be closely examined is the type of conditions that were encountered by people thrown into this situation. Contrary to what some may choose to believe for whatever reason, no one ever wanted to be a slave.

The primary factor motivating the enslaving of Africans, as well as native people of this hemisphere, was profit. The exploitation of resources, be it human or otherwise, meant profits for numerous parties that had few if any regrets about what was happening to the peoples of Turtle Island and Africa. As contacts increased and various European countries jockeyed for positions of advantage, awareness of resources became prominent. The victims of the slave trade were used in many different circumstances. In more warmer climates, the enslaved would toil in agricultural endeavors (sugar, cotton, etc.) In colder environments, there were other labors that would be met. These sometimes included skilled trades such as blacksmithing, carpentry, shoemaking, and sailing. There were other ways of realizing profits in this environment as well. This was to impact the institution of slavery in another way. The fur trade was to prove quite lucrative, as fashion circles in Europe desired the pelts of animals that were prolific at the time in North America. Nations of this continent had been involved with a trade network that was actually hemispheric in scope for centuries. When the trade shifted to demands being established by European business interests, the effect was devastating in the short and long run. Native hunters who originally spent a specific amount of time and traveled to comparative close distances to home now had to range further and further in order to secure hides (deer, beaver, etc.). This was due to the fact that local populations of these animals were being decimated by over hunting. Traveling further meant contact with other people and transiting areas that were under differing custodianship. If protocols were not observed, there was the possibility of conflict. The areas being transited now were to fall victim to heavy trade demands. In addition, men of a respective community were now gone for longer periods of time, which led to a vacuum in the community. Victimizing dark- skinned people by enslavement was nothing new. But enslaving a business asset or members of their community could impact profit negatively. With these factors in mind, enslaving native people on a large scale was bad for business.

These facts didn't necessarily stop the horrors of enslavement, but they played a significant role in keeping down the numbers of victims, at least in the (English) colonies of what is now the eastern United States. For the most part, altruism had nothing to do with it.

In terms of the situations to come after 1492, we must begin to examine the variables involved. For all the horrors suffered by the African ancestors during the period of the Middle Passage, it must be acknowledged that the Trans-Atlantic Slave Trade started in the direction of west to east. The Lucayo Taino, who Columbus encountered on Guanahani, showed him courtesy and hospitality. Indeed, early Spanish reports with the Tainos throughout the Antilles, state time and time again that these people were dignified, gracious hosts, who showed love and harmony among themselves and kindness and respect to those (Spanish) travelers. Perhaps believing that here were possible new trading partners, the people of the islands had initially no reason to suspect an alterior motive. Indeed the presence of items on various Caribbean Islands such as almaizar, a cloth found in areas of Islamic Africa, and guanin, an alloy of gold, silver, and copper that was found in parts of West Africa as well as throughout areas of the Caribbean and Central and South America indicate that oceanic trade was nothing new. The Arawak people (of which the Tainos are a part), as well as other people of Turtle Island and nearby islands, had for centuries ventured to distant destinations not only over land, but by sea. From the numerous islands of the Caribbean to points on the land masses that would later be called North, South, and Central America, it was only a matter of days or in some instances hours to knowledgeable mariners who were aware of sea currents and wind conditions. Certainly, contacts (for example) between Cuba and Florida occurred. Similarities in names of pre-columbian Florida locales and elements of Arawakan vocabulary stand in testament to these regular contacts. Although the number of Arawak seafarers would decline because of social conditions being implemented by the process of colonization, Native American mariners from Florida would continue to travel to various islands and the continent well into the early 1800's. Given this economic reality of trade between the islands and the continent, as well as transoceanic precolumbian contacts with cultures east of the Atlantic, the people of the Antilles probably felt no reason in the beginning to be suspect of these particular sea travelers. Tragically, they would learn differently.

Those original inhabitants of the Bahamas, as well as other islands of the Greater and Lesser Antilles found to their horror that these travelers were not well-intentioned. The kindness extended to these travelers was paid back by the commencement of the Trans- Atlantic Slave Trade and the invasion of the western hemisphere. Estimates range from dozens to hundreds of Tainos being taken from Guanahani alone. As Columbus and his crew landed on other Caribbean Islands, the volume of this human cargo would continue to grow. This enabled Spain to establish a foothold in this hemisphere. Despite the military and diplomatic efforts of Taino leaders such as Coanabo, Guanagacari, and Anacoana (among others), the

Tainos would watch their numbers begin to decline as some of their people were taken across the Atlantic to slave markets in Spain and their scattered outposts on and off the coast of West Africa. Other Tainos would be killed, die from diseases of which they had no immunity, and/or be forced into working in fields and mines. The Spanish began to displace the indigenous culture and economy in the effort to implement their version of civilization. As time went on, Spain and other European countries declared that the Tainos were extinct.

The Tainos suffered horribly, as they were the first to bear the brunt of the invasion. Yet in spite of what has happened, the Tainos refused to cooperate in their own extinction by playing dead. Regardless of constant pressures that have stated that they don't exist, Taino culture survived to the present in locales throughout the Caribbean and found its way again northward to the mainland United States, as well as other places. As the Taino culture struggled to survive in the face of mounting pressure from outside forces and the will of the Carib people (other inhabitants of the Caribbean) was proving to be harder to overcome than anticipated, the colonizers turned to Africa and began to exploit its most valuable resource; the people. And as time went by, other European forces striving to gain military and economic advantages in the hemisphere would also turn to Africa. By the latter part of the nineteenth century, the continent of Africa would suffer the same fate as the areas of Asia and Turtle Island as the land itself was colonized.

As Africans who had been kidnapped and brought to this hemisphere began to arrive, they interacted with Tainos, yet this was not a new phenomenon. Africans, and for that matter numerous other peoples, had made contact with this hemisphere prior to Columbus either intentionally or by accident. The distinction is that because of the event that happened on October 12, 1492, Native Americans and Africans related to each other in an atmosphere of crises. Africans and Native Americans would often come to the aid of each other. Europeans implemented divide and conquer tactics, something that has continued to present times.

The Tainos were certainly no exception. There were reports of Tainos sheltering escaped Africans from many islands. On Borinken (Puerto Rico) in 1502 and 1515, Tainos and Africans united in armed resistance against the Spanish. In a theme that was to be repeated over and over again, European authorities would demand that any future runaways (no matter what their color) must be turned over to them. This was one method of divide and conquer. As the number of escaping Africans seeking to establish free communities in remote locations on various islands grew, surviving Native Americans would be welcomed into these maroon settlements. But these were not the only contacts to occur. In what is now North America, the ill-fated Lucas Vasquez de Allyon Expedition landed in the PeeDee River region of South Carolina in June of 1526. Allyon, a Spaniard, was living on the island of Santo Domingo (Quisqueya/Haiti as it was known to the Tainos). A scouting expedition to this region in 1520 had indicated that this could be a prime location to begin colonization. Spain certainly had already established footholds in the Caribbean, and Central and South America. Consistent with behavior of the time, slaving was a common activity. A man who had been enslaved in 1520 was given the name Ferdinand Chicorana. He accompanied Vasquez de Allyon's expedition in 1526 as an interpreter. Initially located on the coast, the expedition moved inland near a river that was to be believed to be a more favorable location. The settlement, named San Miguel de Guadalupe, was not to last. Bad weather, internal squabbles, disease, and a lack of skills necessary to adapt to the environment spelled doom for the expedition. With the death of Allyon on October 18, a power struggle erupted among the survivors. By this time, the enslaved Africans rebelled by setting fire to some of the structures and fleeing inland, presumably to take their chances among the native population. By this time, Chicorana had already fled into the interior. The remaining survivors headed back to Santo Domingo by December.

Bartolomew De Las Casas, a priest who had spent time in the Caribbean during the early years of Spanish occupation, would be the one to speak in defense of the Tainos. This debate had implications that would impact far beyond the halls of Spanish government. As the invasion of the hemisphere accelerated and one of the largest endeavors in the recorded history of organized crime sanctioned by numerous governments commenced (the Trans- Atlantic Slave Trade), the French, Dutch, British, and Portuguese undertook that part in the saga. They too would face the same set of circumstances, as the two groups of people being victimized were forced to interact with them, for the most part against their will; crises was the circumstance. To determine the humanity of Los Indios while ignoring the humanity of the growing number of kidnapped Africans who found themselves subjected to multiple horrors, the stage was set for the implementation of the strategy of divide and conquer. This strategy was to take on numerous incarnations in the vast areas of the western hemisphere as colonizing entities continually found out members of the indigenous population and escaping Africans more often than not would come to the assistance of each other. As long as the two groups of people could be kept at odds, the chances for any particular colonizer of expanding its sphere of influence stood a better chance of succeeding. Those of the oppressed who lost their sense of dignity in the onslaught of seemingly endless physical and psychic pressures may have attempted to gain favor in the eyes of the oppressors. There would be times when these tactics were successful. And although the number of enslaved people in the Americas (especially North America) would increasingly take on the physical characteristics representing a rainbow of African peoples, it is a fact that along with the theft of massive tracks of land from Turtle Island, a sizable portion of the indigenous people native to this continent were assimilated into the system of chattel slavery. When examining the colonial period of what is now the United States, records are found regularly referring to slaves who were red as well as black. Legislation passed by governing bodies throughout the colonies make reference to "negro, Indian, mulatto, and mustee slaves". When escapes occurred, posters made reference that the escapee (in some instances) were "Indian looking".

Places like Charleston, South Carolina, became known for the importation of Africans and rum, as well as the exportation of native people, who usually were condemned to exile and horror in numerous Caribbean locations. As it turned out, South Carolina would become known as the colony in North America that had kidnapped and enslaved numerically the largest amount of native people. There existed for a time an umbilical relationship between Barbados and South Carolina. Both areas were pivotal in the efforts of England to maintain a strong presence in the hemisphere. Sugar, which was a resource of the island, became a main export item to the mainland. As part of a cycle, timber from the Carolinas was found to be crucial in the rum making process. Food items such as beef and pork, which were herded on the mainland, found their way to Barbados. By the 1640s, this reciprocal relationship was firmly established. British expatriates began to search out new opportunities that existed on the mainland. The most profitable commodity was human beings. Early on during the slave trade, some native peoples from the Caribbean ended up on the continent, where they were to suffer their fates. A pattern developed that saw the importation of kidnapped Africans into Charleston, and the export of kidnapped Native Americans out of the same location. The intermarriage between African men and native women that occurred would produce children of mixed ancestry. This was happening because of the low numbers of African women who were not being kidnapped (at first). As the number of African kidnap victims increased over time and ended up in the western hemisphere, these children would intermarry with an increasing pool of people. That led to the fact that most victims suffering under slavery would phenotypically have predominate African features. As much as some that champion ethnic purity want to believe, it is rare that any culture and people live in isolation from each other. People have interacted in a number of ways as long as there has been humanity. Attempts at categorizing people into restricted ethnic and racial categories for the sake of sociopolitical exploitation, continue to distort the truth and stifle any objective discussions when it comes to examining historical and contemporary social phenomenon.

As white racist dogma and governmental racial policies increasingly dominated life in North America, indigenous people found themselves under attack, legislative and otherwise, for being allegedly African (and this continues to be the case today). When early colonial records are examined that relate to the states of various native groups, there are constant references that seem to imply the concerns on the behalf of the different colonizing entities. Thomas Jefferson, an individual who contributed in his own way to the mixing of gene pools, is quoted as saying when speaking of the Pamunkey of Virginia, "The Pamunkies are reduced to about ten or twelve men, tolerably pure from mixture with other colors". Of the Mattaponi also of Virginia he stated, "There remains of the Mattaponies three or four men only, and have more negro than Indian Blood". As there came a larger percentage of Africans who had been victimized, many colonizing entities characterized and recorded the slave population as "negro" and mulatto. The slaveholding class were of a disposition that felt it would be necessary to equate "slave" with "black" (anyone with any degree of African ancestry). Native peoples of the hemisphere were to suffer from the same type of indignities perpetuated by the ruling classes on those of African descent. Through the use of legislation and the manipulating of terminology, many native people were legislated-"out of sight, out of mind", as laws put on the books effectively obscured their existence over and over again.

The trafficking of indigenous people had firmly taken hold by this point in time (1700's). Various colonial entities, be they Spanish, French, or British, had their hands in this form of commerce. Native American peoples had been involved in forms of slavery. Colonizers would begin to exploit this situation time and time again. In some instances, playing off different nations against each other became the order of the day. As tribal warfare occurred (which was hardly a new situation) slaving became one of the side effects of these actions. During this same time-frame and into the nineteenth century, similar circumstances would continue to happen in Africa. Those nations of people who were not capable of strong defense fell victim to the predations of those nations that proved militarily powerful. On both sides of the Atlantic Ocean, nations would cause war on each other for whatever reason, and the losers (if they lived) would find themselves as part of a slave caravan. In Florida, there were many Christian Indians living near Catholic missions. Prior to the coming of Europeans to this part of Turtle Island, the area called Ikanyuska by some of its indigenous inhabitants was the home of several strong nations of people. In the northwestern part which would in another era be known as the Panhandle, lived the Apalachees. The northeast and central part of the peninsular was home to the Timucua. The Calusa occupied the southwestern area from approximately the Tampa Bay area extending down into the Keys. The southeastern area was the location of the Tequesta.

These were the dominant nations on the peninsula, although smaller nations were also present such as the Guales, Ais, and Tocobaga (as well as others). As the Spanish made their impact felt on the area over a period of two centuries, changes came to many of the inhabitants. Some of those that survived warfare, as well as unknown diseases, adapted to Christianity, but did so at a price. Having to one degree or another forsaken (some) of their traditions, these people were easy targets for the slaughter. These settlements for all-extensive purposes were defenseless, as the men were forbidden by the clergy to have weapons, especially firearms. Indeed, these native people in some instances had come to these missions not necessarily seeking salvation as much as the need for physical protection. At many of these locations there would sometimes be a small garrison of Spanish soldiers. These troops however, proved to be no match for well armed, numerically superior forces. Converted Apalachees, Timucua, Guale, and Calusa fell to the persistent onslaughts of war parties that not only carried traditional weaponry, but guns as well. Ironically, there had been a time when some of these nations had commanded respect by neighboring nations because of the prowess of their warriors. Yamasee (who themselves would later be victimized by slaving expedition), Appalachicola, Yuchi, Creek, and Chickasaw warriors became feared for hundreds of miles throughout the southeastern coastal regions and the interior. At times these native warriors would be accompanied by Europeans who had a direct stake in the capture of people who were to suffer the fate of enslavement. In the 1670s and 80s, the Goose Creek Men, a group of expatriate British Barbadians based in South Carolina near their namesake body of water, came to specialize in these types of endeavors. While the initial pursuit of these entrepreneurs was to seek trade with various nations of the southeast, it was soon discovered that humans were just as valuable a commodity as any trade good. The legacy of the Goose Creek Men was to continue as slavers carried out their endeavors into the 1800s. They certainly were not the only ones looking for these types of opportunities, just as the peoples of Florida were hardly unique as far as being victimized. Many small and not so small nations over a wide geographical area such as the Choctaw, Stono, Tuscarora, Pedee, Santee, Yazoo, Caddo, and Pawnee (to name a few) would find themselves in the merciless path of slaving expeditions, as the English, French and Spanish would continue to fan the flames of animosity between Native Americans, and work these situations to their own advantage. Similar to what some Africans involved in slaving exploits found out to their misfortune, if the count on war captives was too small, the slavers would become the enslaved along with their victims.

Spanish slavers certainly had established themselves with their operations in the southeast. Native peoples were kidnapped as targets of opportunity. In 1521 numbers of indigenous people from what is now called coastal South Carolina were taken to be enslaved in the Caribbean. Those who had the misfortune of encountering Hernando De Soto suffered similar fates if they were not killed in any number of confrontations that marked his expedition. From 1539 through 1543, this expedition which landed first in Florida, then traveled through what is now Georgia, South Carolina, Mississippi, Arkansas, Texas, and Louisiana. The Timucua in Florida were the first to encounter this expedition. They were the first and certainly not the last to put up armed resistance once it was clear that this was an incursion, not merely an adventure of exploration. Ancestors of what are now identified as Cherokee, Creek, Choctaw, and Chickasaw as well as others of the southeast (if they could not escape quickly enough), would be forced into slavery after suffering defeat. Similar to what had happened in the wake of later English slaving ventures, further disaster would strike and continue to decimate populations over vast regions. In what could be described as biological warfare, diseases to which most indigenous peoples of the hemisphere had no immunity, struck population after population. A Spaniard named Tristan De Luna led an expedition into Florida and Georgia in 1559. Juan Pardo, another Spaniard, led an expedition into South Carolina in 1566. These expeditions, happening years after that of DeSoto's journeys, found village after village that had been greatly reduced in numbers. Reports from DeSoto's era had described these settlements as prosperous and numerous. Now, the surviving residents were refugees rebuilding their lives.

Yet there were other ways in which slave merchants would engage in kidnapping on whatever scale. Slaving activity was not restricted to the southeast. Spanish interests capitalized on rivalries of native nations in what is now the southwest United States, as well as Central and South America. The southeastern United States may have seen the most intense activity in this horrific endeavor (in what is now North America), but it was hardly unique. Prior to the point of contact that occurred with Henry Hudson in the area now known as New York

City and the adjacent areas of New Jersey in 1609, smaller communities of people along the northeast Atlantic Coast realized quickly that when masted ships appeared close to the shores of their settlements, people tended to disappear and not return. English, Spanish, and Portuguese ships had transited waters off of the northeastern coasts since 1497. It was not uncommon for slaving ships to travel to coastal communities that were isolated because of distance from other communities. These communities were not necessarily aware (initially) of the fact that these maritime vessels spelled trouble. People in whatever numbers would travel out to these vessels to establish communication, usually in the hopes of establishing some sort of trade relationship. When it was determined that there was a sufficient number of people who would prove profitable at a later date, the ship would simply sail away. This ploy proved successful for at least two centuries on coastal regions along Africa and throughout what is now called the Americas. Oral histories were related by descendants of enslaved Africans in the United States that told of tales of horror as their respective ancestors were tricked into becoming kidnap victims. Specifically, these stories were told to writers from the WPA who interviewed elderly people of African, and African/Native descent during the 1930s, who had lived during the last years of the slave era in the United States. Ironically, when investigating the timeline of these stories, it becomes clear that some of the ancestors of the interviewees who were kidnap victims from Africa experienced these horrors after the importation of "slaves" was supposedly outlawed in the United States in 1807.

A Patauxet man named Tisquantum, who would become known to the Pilgrims as Squanto, experienced firsthand the horrors of the slave trade. Kidnapped in 1614 by British slavers, he at first was taken to England and eventually ended up in Spain, where he was eventually freed because of the intervention of Spanish priests. Working his way back to England, he managed from there to work his way back to what is now called Massachusetts by 1619, only to find that his entire community had succumbed to disease that lingered after the European slavers had departed. It was only days after Pilgrims landed at what they called Plymouth Rock when a native man approached and greeted them in English. After the shock had worn off, the Pilgrims were to learn that this man had been taught to speak words of English by Tisquantim. Records from the days of Puritan occupation in Massachusetts make reference to native people who had fallen victim to slavery. Court documents of 1636 mention that Chousop, the "Indian of Black Island", was to be kept as a slave for life to work. On July 20, 1676, in an area known as Bridgewater, Massachusetts, the wife and son of Metacom, known as King Philip to the English, were captured during the war named after him and sold into slavery in the Caribbean. The French managed to victimize some peoples from the interior of North America, such as the Pawnee. For centuries, the Spanish (after victimizing the Taino of the Caribbean) continued to traffic in human beings of the western hemisphere, victimizing various people in the southwestern United States, as well as Central and South America. Once Spanish domination had ceased in these areas, the remaining colonizers kept up the legacy. Where the outright enslavement of people has largely ceased in modern times, other forms of oppression have substituted. Indigenous peoples in South America have been shot in remote areas of their respective countries by agents of military dictatorships. As late as the early 1900s there were reports of slavery in various parts of Central and South America.

No doubt that there has been an emphasis on the collaboration of African and native People in the Trans-Atlantic Slave Trade. While it is true that Africans played a part in the slave trade in Africa and native people in the western hemisphere mirrored this kind of involvement, it must be ascertained that given the zeal displayed by the primary perpetrators in this sad saga, the trafficking of human beings was going to be a reality, regardless there was involvement of Africans and Native Americans as partners in the trafficking. The perpetrators proved time and time again how resourceful they could be to maintain their endeavors, and they would not hesitate to go to whatever length to preserve this perversion.

Collaboration on the part of some did not form the main structure of the slave trade. People, and specifically the sons and daughters of Africa as well as Turtle Island, were seen as a means to an end. Lives were (in the minds of the slaveholding class and their support systems) dehumanized. This was the justification for the theft of land and for the exploitation of the bodies and minds of millions of people. A combination of legislative, religious, and military actions (not necessarily in this order) saw to it that there was no turning back from this path of exploitation. Land and natural resources were to be taken, and those calling the shots needed people to labor so that they could reap the benefits, regardless of horrific suffering that was a direct result. The need to exploit was relentless and devious in these goals. This instance meant obtaining human beings so their life energy could be used to fulfill the conquerors' vision of the world.

Exploring on the behalf of France, Giovanni da Verrazano sailed into the lower part of what is now New York Harbor in 1524. Henry Hudson ventured into the region during 1609 to sail up a river that now is identified with his name. While there was no gold to be found as in other parts of the hemisphere, the northeastern region was rich in fur-bearing animals. This fact would make up for the shortage in some types of furs no longer available in Europe, such as beaver. Enterprising Dutch, French, and British, were to begin to saturate the northeast from the coast to the Great Lakes in pursuit of this treasure. Waterways proved to be the highways of the era, something the native peoples had known and utilized for centuries. Rivers such as the Saint Lawrence, Hudson, Mohawk, Niagara, and their tributaries interlocked to provide excellent means of travel for those strong enough to journey on them. Trading posts began to appear in locations in the interior, as well as along the coasts. These included New Amsterdam (Lower Manhattan), Fort Orange (now Albany, New York), Montreal, Niagara, Michilimackinac, and Detroit (among others). Native Americans were an intregal part of these endeavors. Peoples such as the Mahican, Wiechquaeskeck, Huron, Ottawa, Nipissing, Cree, Potawatomi, Chippewa, Mohawk, and Seneca were just some of the key players in the unfolding drama that was the race for economic and political control of what was being called by Europeans the "New World". While this was happening in the northeast, other chapters continued to unfold in the mid-Atlantic region, the southeast, Caribbean, and South and Central America. In May of 1624, early Dutch colonists arrived in Manhattan. This group was comprised of thirty families and some merchants. At the time, the governor was Cornelius Jacobsen May. He was to be followed (in the governor's capacity) by Peter Miniut. In his capacity as governor of the Dutch colony of New Netherlands, he supposedly purchased Manhattan for twenty four dollars in 1626. This outpost was named New Amsterdam. Their seat was at the lower end of this island. Settlers were to spread out in areas that encompassed parts of what is now New York City (Bronx, Brooklyn, Staten Island), New Jersey, and Westchester County. Adriaen van der Donck was a Dutchman who had land in what is now called the Bronx (New York) in the 1640s. He had cordial relationships with the native people of the area. At times, he would visit some of the settlements. He observed that in war "They seldom destroy women and children unless it be in their first fury, the women they treat as their own, and the children they bring up as their own to strengthen the nation".

In 1638 William Kieft became governor of New Amsterdam. During his tenure in the post of governor, relationships with the Algonquin peoples of the region deteriorated. During the early years of Dutch presence, the Dutch West India Company had instructed its representatives in New Netherlands to stay on good terms with all of the native people. Settlement was (at first) discouraged so the fur trade could take hold. Some native men were employed as guides into interior regions to obtain furs. Good relations not only had economic reasons. The Dutch relied heavily on the native people for food, be it meat, fish, or agricultural products. By the time Kieft took over, settlers were coming into the region in larger numbers. As some of the native people fell to disease, Dutch settlers pushed out into native lands to build farms. Many of the native peoples found they no longer could readily access areas that had been theirs to transit historically. Misunderstandings grew from cultural differences, and violence flared with increasing frequency and casualties on both sides. The native peoples began to distrust many of the Dutch. To say that Keift held the native people of the area in low regard would be an understatement. He would have been rid of them if possible. In February of 1643, he saw a chance to do so. A group of Wiechquaeskeck People had fled from a war party of Mohicans who were from the area of present-day Albany. The refugees had arrived in the vicinity of the New Amsterdam settlement in late January of 1643. Initially, they were given food by the some of the Dutch settlers, as they had fled with little heading southward in the middle of winter. Some were to establish a camp at Corlears Hook (where the base of the Manhattan Bridge now is located in Manhattan), and some established a camp across the Hudson River at Pavonia (present-day Jersey City). Under orders from Keift, these refugees were attacked in their sleep. The result was a massacre. In the weeks that followed, there were other military actions taken against other local native peoples in the immediate area, including Staten Island and Long Island (this is in the area today known as Brooklyn and Queens). What happened as a result was that a majority of Algonquin peoples rose up against the Dutch. As far north as southern Connecticut and along the Hudson

Valley, Dutch farms came under attack as war parties set out to retaliate against the wrongs committed against them. Kieft realized he had only a small number of soldiers to deal with the situation. These were not soldiers of the Dutch Army, but mercenaries in the employment of the Dutch West India Company. They were a mixture of German, British, and Dutch. Fighting would continue into 1645, covering parts of Connecticut, Long Island (including Queens and Brooklyn), and present-day Westchester County. And though many Dutch Men had firearms, they were not trained soldiers by any stretch of the imagination.

Wall Street in lower Manhattan, New York City, is recognized today as a center for financial transactions that impact national and international trends. Wall Street actually began as a defensive perimeter barrier to keep angry Algonquin warriors out of the Dutch settlement at the southern tip of the island. And while Kieft appealed to the British in southern New England for help, mercenary forces would eventually aid New Amsterdam. Some of these men were led by John Underhill, someone who had gained a reputation for attacking native settlements with a particularly vicious zeal. He would enhance his reputation further on Long Island and in present-day Westchester County. One of the horrors in which Underhill took part in was the setting aflame of a Wecquasqueek village at Pound Ridge (Westchester County), in March of 1644. It is believed that more than five hundred people died in the flames. Underhill had prior experience in implementing this tactic, as he had done the same thing to a Pequot Village in Connecticut in May of 1637. Kieft also gave land grants to formerly enslaved Africans. There was no animosity between the native population and Africans (of any status) at the time. There had been no reports of Africans participating in the raiding parties that perpetrated the massacres at Corlears Hook and Pavonia. The total size of the grants encompassed an area that by contemporary standards stretched from Canal Street to 34th Street in lower Manhattan. Kieft had created a buffer zone as a guard against attacks that might come from northern Manhattan. By 1645, peace was re-established. The attack(s) anticipated from the direction of northern Manhattan never came, and there are no reports of any of these homes established of freed Africans ever being attacked by any native war party. Over time, some Algonquin and some Iroqouis communities were to adopt enslaved Africans. These refugees willing to risk making their way into the interior regions of the northeast found themselves in a situation better than those left behind. Those who successfully escaped assimilated into the respective culture of their new hosts. Similarly, interactions took on various forms within European settlements as well. For example, excavation of slave burial grounds in New York City would continue not only to yield African bodies, but native bodies as well.

Many people who had not been captured initially for the purpose of enslavement were the numerous Algonquin peoples of the northeast. These captives were survivors of the many battles that happened where the native nations of the area felt the only way of dealing with the English settlers was war. Yet the result was the same, lifelong enslavement. We will probably never know the exact numerical figure of those Mashantucket, Wampanoag, Narragansett, Mohegan,

Nipmuc, or any other peoples of this region who found themselves in the hold of slave vessels heading toward the Caribbean. Even in this region however, there had been slaving activity during the 1500s and 1600s carried out by sea vessels that looked for targets of opportunity. A pattern emerged as those who survived such encounters would exodus to wherever it was felt some degree of safety would be had. These survivors would often be absorbed into larger groups of people. Prior to the coming of Europeans in 1492, those individuals who found themselves alive after a skirmish and in the capture of whatever people would experience execution (depending on if the basis for the battle to begin with was for expansion or revenge) or enslavement. Yet along areas of what was to become the eastern United States, a slave may eventually end up being adopted into the nation that had captured him or her to begin with. This was the case where the initial purpose of the raid was to replace members of a nation who may have died for whatever reason (warfare, disease, etc.). In some other instances such as among southeastern people an individual might remain a slave but intermarry into a nation. The children of such a union would be born free. In various parts of Africa, a slave could hold property and rise to a social status that demanded respect. Under these circumstances, being a slave was not necessarily a pariah. With the possible exception of early French New Orleans, upward mobility of enslaved persons was unthinkable in areas under European control after 1492. With the invasion of the hemisphere chattel slavery was to become the order of the day. Thus, the demand for slaves became insatiable. Over a period of centuries, while not rivaling in number the horrific trafficking in Africans, the kidnapping of Native Americans would continue. The pattern of keeping women and children and exporting of men had a practical logic. These individuals may still be in some proximity to their home grounds, even if the distance was a question of several hundred miles. If these individuals or a group of them escaped, there was a real possibility of making their way back to familiar surroundings. This is the advantage of being on or relatively near one's own turf, in a manner of speaking.

There was also the added dimension that in the immediate area other native people(s) whose warriors may have been responsible to whatever degree in the kidnapping and enslavement process may dwell. There was also the very real possibility that a mature male, given some of the aforementioned variables, could make for a dangerous adversary, especially if he escaped.

Certainly, as the colonizers would find out, Africans could be equally as hazardous if they escaped. The difference here, however, was that an escaped African did not necessarily have a thorough knowledge of the land, something that could prove a liability if being pursued by slave catchers. This situation was to change in varying degrees after the War of Independence in the 1770s. Africans who had accompanied white traders into the various territories would come to be familiar with the lay of the land. Also, the British would arm enslaved Africans and promise freedom to anyone who fought for their cause. This was done to place a buffer against the colonists militarily, as well as become a thorn in the side of the colonial military machine. After the War of Independence, some of these armed men of African descent would continue guerilla actions in the name of the British Crown in the vicinity of the Savannah River over a period of years. Out of concern for this situation with traders transiting native communities in the interior and elsewhere after the war, some southern states passed laws forbidding traders against taking anyone of African descent into territories where contact could be made with large segments of the native population. This was easily said on paper, but it was another thing to enforce. Traders would continue to use men of African descent during their ventures into the interior. At the same time men of African descent who had been armed and promised freedom by the British, also found they now had a degree of familiarity with large tracts of territory. Such an individual or group of people would prove dangerous indeed if their lives were on the line. After the birth of the Unites States, many men of African descent headed for the territories of various indigenous nations. The irony here is that no doubt some of these men had mixed ancestry, given the nature of slavery in the colonies. Some of these escapees may have been traveling to communities where they had bloodlines. While this may appear to be a phenomenon that happened in the southeastern area of what is now the United States, similar events were happening, and continued to happen throughout the eastern seaboard and wherever enslaved people took a chance for freedom.

Those victims of raids who survived an attack on their homes, or those who were kidnaped outright, were to suffer further trauma. The main result was those women and children still alive after raids would find themselves in the slave markets of the eastern seaboard. The destinations after this would often be any number of colonial settlements. This set the stage for the meeting of men from Africa and women of Turtle Island in the slave quarters. For a span of time during the earlier years of the Trans-Atlantic Slave Trade, there was a shortage of African women being imported into this hemisphere. Native American men who were still alive after falling victim to slave raids would be taken to a coastal port such as Charleston and within a short amount of time, they would end up in the hold of a slave ship bound for any number of ports in the Caribbean, or in some instances, Europe or Africa. Thus, for those African men now enslaved as well as those native women in the same predicament, there was little choice as far as having a partner was concerned (or anything else, for that matter). In the post 1492 era, this situation gave rise to people of multiple ancestry. A boy or girl being born in the slave quarters would have an African father and a Native American mother. This was new only in that these children were born into slavery. These types of births had also occurred since before the hemispheric invasion in the numerous settlements, where Africans would be adopted into various nations, or in those situations where African travelers such as merchants and marooned sailors took native women as wives into their own settlements, be it in what is now North, South, or Central America. In some other areas of the hemisphere, indigenous women who had witnessed the devastation of their communities found that the selection of partners had been narrowed drastically. Thus, some women would have little choice but to look outside of traditional structures and seek partners from other races. New England is one example as Algonquin women of various nations married African as well as European men. These circumstances led to any number of dynamics taking place. Many native cultures in the western hemisphere and especially in what is now the eastern United States were matrilineal. This was not usually the case where the father of a child was not native. Because of matrilineal affiliations, a child in native settlements would have ties to a specific clan that would be able to aid in the upbringing of that child within a stable social setting, although the threat of warfare and slavery would continue to exist up through the 1800s. Unfortunately, speculation is the source for the most part in determining what it was like for a child born into more Afrocentric settings because of the lack of written history in regards to the early settlements in this hemisphere, pre-or post- columbian (that is, specific influences and retention outside of the confines of enslavement). There are some exceptions. For example, an examination of some cultures that have survived with what may be obvious retention may give testimony. Garifuna communities are a possible source, as well as contemporary settlements of maroon descendants in the Caribbean, and Central and South America. While there have been retention of aspects of indigenous and African interaction in Native and African American communities throughout the hemisphere, it is more difficult to pinpoint the origins. The possible exception here is in households today, where family members (conscientiously or otherwise) keep elements of both cultures alive as part of their respective lifestyles. In the setting of chattel slavery, racial and ethnic distinction were blurred, only to be kept alive in the memories of the parents. A child growing to maturity under these circumstances may have retained elements of what was taught to him or her by each parent. This same individual would also have to cope with the immediate circumstances slavery dictated. There was always the possibility of being sold away. The cruelties of this institution demanded its own set of priorities. Thus the knowledge of the origins of one's own worldview could have very well been lost, or as the case may be, kept alive through oral tradition with the risk of something being lost in the telling (although written history, too, falls victim to this).

Given the reality of enslavement, there was little choice as far as choosing life partners were concerned, or anything else for that matter. As time passed, the progeny of these unions, as well as other unions comprised the slave population. Breeding became a priority, especially after the importation of Africans became illegal in the United States in 1807 (slavers managed to find ways around this law, and the importation of Africans would continue). The horror of slavery was further mutated as women of color were selected for the specific task of bearing children; "breeders". These children were not always the result of both parents being of dark skin tones. Some slaveholders used women of color as nothing more than vehicles for producing products destined for the auction block. The enslaved class in actuality, was comprised of people that, in fact, could have been of pure African or native blood. Many enslaved people by this time were of varying degrees of multiple ancestry. In cases where slaves had managed to retain their native culture to some extent, there was the possibility of finding the way home, no matter how remote the chance. This was the case where the enslaved were kept on the continent as opposed to being shipped to the Caribbean. The escapee(s) had to risk the fact that there might not have been remnants of his or her people to return to. If one could not find his or her own people for whatever reason, there existed the possibility of being adopted by friendly nations. As some indigenous nations became increasingly aware of the nature of chattel slavery, they would look out for the welfare community members when outsiders were present, including community members of mixed ancestry, or where members of the community who had been fully adopted into the society were of African ancestry. The Shawnee are just one example. There were negotiations held at Fort Pitt in October of 1775 between an American delegation and representatives of the Maquachake Shawnee. Cornstalk, a prominent leader agreed to return all captives held among the Shawnee, be they black or white. He refused to turn over the offspring of a Shawnee man and a black woman because of the real possibility of enslavement. At the siege of Boonesborough Kentucky in 1778, Black Fish, a leader of the Chalahgawtha Shawnee relied on the language skills of Pompey. This man was believed to be an escaped, enslaved African who had been living among the Shawnee for more than ten years (at that point in time). Pompey interpreted for Black Fish in talks between himself (Black Fish) and Daniel Boone prior to the siege where Shawnee warriors surrounded and isolated the fort over a two-day period.

The people who were to be eventually known as Seminoles are a highly documented example of unity (initially). During the initial period of colonization and then as the United States would start and continue to spread over the continent, many Native Americans had the opportunity to see for themselves what the condition of chattel slavery meant. These same observers no doubt also watched other Native Americans who had been enslaved working alongside African co-victims. At this point in time many slaves would have been of varying degrees of racial mixtures. But red and black aiding each other was not exclusive to the Shawnee or Seminole. In spite of the numerous tactics the ruling class used to create animosity with varying degrees of success, there continued to be situations where Africans and Native Americans continued to look out for each other.

On various islands of the Caribbean Apalachees, Pequots, Cherokees, Yamasees, Creeks, Tainos, Choctaws, Cusabos, Timucuas, and men from other nations (some of which have been lost in the sands of time) now found themselves enslaved with men and women from Africa, Central and South America, and, in some instances, Asia. Similar circumstances existed in other locations such as Cape Verde off the west coast of Africa. The islands were becoming a melting pot of dozens of cultures forced together under horrific circumstances. In the Caribbean, this was to give rise (along with Eurocentric elements) to cultures now identified as West Indian, Puerto Rican, Cuban, Dominican, etc. Yet as dire and hopeless as these situations may have seen, the human spirit would time and time again call for resistance. On the islands of the Caribbean (as well as throughout the hemisphere), this was no exception. Africans by the dozens against all odds escaped to remote regions. In some instances, they would be taken in and adopted by indigenous communities. After the indigenous populations declined throughout the islands, more and more of the maroon communities would take on an Afrocentric atmosphere. In these communities, Native Americans, in some instances survivors of the original population(s), would be welcomed. In Central and South America similar circumstances were taking place. In Suriname, some native warriors that had originally been hired to hunt down runaway Africans would join forces with them. In Portuguese Brazil, native warriors were instrumental in the destruction of numbers of quilombos from the 1500s through the 1700s (quilombos were communities formed by escaped slaves and their descendants). Yet even here colonial authorities realized all to well that it was just as likely to find Africans and indigenous peoples forming alliances. It is true that at times indigenous people would kill Africans and vice versa. Colonial authorities throughout the Americas and Caribbean constantly engaged in efforts to make African and indigenous peoples antagonistic toward each other as much as possible. At times this meant that alliances that had been cemented were demolished because of bribes and/or friction among factions of the people. The larger nations of the southeastern United States are but one study in this. But divisiveness was not always the scenario. It seems that when red and black encountered each other in the bush, at times, it was realized that there were differences that could be respected, as well as commonalities to be shared. During the 1600s, in the Pernambuco region of Brazil existed the nation state of Palmares. It is believed that this community or, more accurately, coalition of communities, began around 1605 to 1606 and would last until 1695. While Afrocentric culturally, there is evidence that indigenous people were a part of the population. Other quilombos of varying sizes could be found throughout Brazil. Often, the inhabitants crossed racial and ethic lines. Jaguaripe was one such settlement located near Bahia. This community consisted of Tupinamba People and escaped Africans. It is believed to have existed from the late 1500s into 1620s. Similar to other parts of the hemisphere, the Portuguese continued to find Africans residing in indigenous settlements. In 1706, the Portuguese passed a law stating that "blacks, mixed bloods and slaves" were not allowed in the backcountry region for fear of them joining in alliances with indigenous people hostile to the colony. In Panama, when Francis Drake began to harass the Spanish, he enlisted the aid of maroons from what is now known as Darien, Quarequa Province. The warriors of this community were indigenous as well as African. The roots of these communities could pre date the arrival of the Spanish, as Balboa had encountered African men who were prisoners of a local village at the time of his explorations in this region in 1519. It was explained to Balboa that these men were from a community within several days' journey, and had been feuding with this settlement for some time. Out of necessity, these settlements had to be capable of defending themselves by whatever strategy. Some of these maroon communities were more than able to hold their own against incursions of colonial forces. As mentioned before Palmares, lasted throughout the 1600s. It was after the end of the Dutch-Portuguese War in 1654 that the towns of Palmares began to fight off military expeditions on the average of every 15 months, eventually succumbing to force in January 1695 as its capital city,

Macaco, fell. In Mexico, during the period of 1560 to 1580 in the regions of Guanajanto, Guadalajara, and Zacetecas, Africans who had escaped from slavery united with the local indigenous populations to wreak havoc on Spanish businesses and settlements. By the beginning of the 1600s in the area between Vera Cruz and Orizaba, some of the maroon communities became so strong that the Spanish sought to negotiate for terms of peace. From the Spanish perspective things had become so hazardous that there was a constant danger when traveling from place to place. It was reported time and time again that multiracial bands of guerrillas had rendered travel between Vera Cruz and Mexico City almost impossible unless accompanied by large numbers of soldiers. It was in the Vera Cruz region that the community led by a leader known as Yanga reached terms that would lead to the founding of the town, "San Lorenzo de los Negroes", around 1610. Northeast Mexico would become home to Seminoles and other relocated southeastern peoples who had fled unstable conditions in Oklahoma. As the early decades of the 1800s progressed, forces of the then young United States of America headed south into Florida, they learned there would always be a price to pay when attacking Seminole settlements, no matter what the complexion of the inhabitants. By this time throughout North America it had also been observed that Native Americans would aid and/or assist Africans in other ways. When native warriors would attack white settlements, often Africans would be left unharmed, or taken back to native communities. This gave rise to divide and conquer tactics by Europeans colonists throughout the hemisphere, as it was realized that when left to their own devices, more often than not, Africans and Native Americans would come to the aid of each other. As time went by, some Native American men who had been taken from areas of the eastern Atlantic seaboard (as well as Central and South America) and forced into slavery would find their way to these maroon communities if they were resourceful enough to escape their captors. It is difficult to know how many of these men were able to do this. As many of these settlements had a district Afrocentric atmosphere, elements of the culture that may have been retained were probably absorbed into the larger (Afrocentric) culture. It must be noted, however, that the culture(s) of these maroon communities were multi faceted as the Africans represented numerous traditions, be it Yoruba, Akan, Wolof, Fon, Ibo, Bambara, etc., because the Africans themselves originated from different points of the African continent. The Caribs, another people that had occupied parts of the Antilles had (also) had contact and interaction with African peoples both before and after 1492. It was among settlements of the Caribs in the Caribbean that the cloth almaizar had been found. This fabric was common throughout Islamic Africa (north and south of the Sahara). Was this material obtained by direct or indirect trade? Whatever the origin, the term "Black Carib" is heard increasingly as numerous European elements jockeyed for control of the Caribbean.

The question comes up of what the enslaved looked like. To the popular mindset the term "slave" automatically means "black". But this was not necessarily the case. At times an escaped slave was a Native American, or the progeny of a man and woman that were of African and Native ancestry, or any number of racial combinations. Women of color were seen as nothing more than property in the eyes of the slaveholding class. The master of the house/plantation felt it was open season on women, especially slaves. Women, regardless of color, were oppressed during these times in varying degrees. Notices of runaways would often state that an individual was "Indian looking", or believed to be headed for Indian Country. It was economically and socially convenient to enslave or project the image of a slave as being anyone dark. In a society where those in control sought to exploit and in an environment that was (is) intensely racialized, numerous terms to describe people of mixed ancestry. "Mulatto, mustee, mestizo, zambo, quadroon, octaroon, pardo," etc. If the situation called for it, the enslaved could be Native American. If this native had African ancestry to some degree, he/she would be an automatic target for enslavement. Overall, this mentality of the "One Drop Rule" exists in the twenty first century. To have African ancestry supposedly negates and supersedes any other ancestry an individual may have. From the vantage point of the twenty first century, many have worked hard to demonstrate that African heritage is one to be proud of. Those that have championed this sense of pride certainly had predecessors that in prior years, did the same against massive adversity. Black pride counters racist attitudes that at times continue to negatively impact any ancestry mixed with African. During the era of slavery, it was this racist ideology of the One Drop Rule that guaranteed there would be no shortage of a population that could be victimized. In the United States, during the era of legal segregation, this furthered the aims and desires of those championing white supremacy who longed to see African Americans continually degraded, and denied what was rightfully theirs. Regardless of the timeframe, there has always existed a mind set that relentlessly examined any situation where there is a mixture of African bloodlines. 'Are they Negroes with Indian blood?' Those Seminole Indian Negro Scouts found themselves and their families caught up in a bureaucratic quagmire of federal agencies over the question of giving them land in exchange for their services fighting people of the southern plains and outlaws along the Texas-Mexican border. It seems the way that the United States Government managed to get these Seminoles out of Mexico and into Texas to work for government interests was the promise of land. As fate would have it, this unit was one of the most highly decorated units in the history of the United States Army. They never suffered a fatality in combat. In a scenario with which most Native Americans are too familiar with (as well as most communities of color) the United States Government never honored their agreement to these warriors and their families. The Scouts and their families, with the exception of a handful of elderly Seminole people, would be evicted from lands they lived on (in southern Texas) while the men of the community had been fighting for the United States by 1914. In British colonies, and later the United States, state and federal representatives constantly would sought to prove that a native community "were Negroes". Wherever a native community (has) had instances of African intermarriage, the trouble quotient was (is) always close at hand. This could (can) take the form of those communities being denied resources from government agencies (in the

United States when a said community is not "recognized") or having outside interests use existing resources and property by whatever means from communities they have determined are not "real Indians". Thus these outside interests attempt to justify their actions by dictating to a community what an "Indian" should look like, and that "look" is what serves the long, and short, range goals of that outside entity. At the same time, given the pressures of living in an environment of racial animosity of varying degrees and intensity, some African Americans use the "One Drop" mentality to add sociopolitical strength by numbers. Those of African/Native ancestry who pay homage to both sides of their ancestry (as opposed to paying lip service) are sometimes looked upon with suspicion, either by those who feel that there is a denial of Africaness, and/or by those who see it as a denial of their roots on Turtle Island.

At the time of Spanish and later English contacts with the region, the area now called North Carolina was home to numerous people who spread from the coastal lowlands into the Appalachian Mountains. People of the coastal and lowlands included the Hatteras, Pamlico, Meherrin, Cape Fear, Chowanocs, Pasquotanks, Poteskeets, Matchapungas, Nottoway, and Tuscarora. At one point, the Tuscarora were a dominate presence in the region. They had fifteen major settlements, and there was a time when their influence extended from the coastal shore to the base of the mountains in the west (of North Carolina). There, relations with whites were at first friendly. Tuscaroras at times allied with whites to fight other native people. But disease began to take its toll by the early 1700s as it had been happening to other communities throughout the hemisphere. The Tuscaroras by this time were victims of increased slave raids into their communities as well. Many of their numbers were subject to other forms of abuse coming from the English colonists. By 1711 these circumstances were to lead to war as Tuscaroras set out to avenge the wrongs that were being perpretrated against them. They had allies such as Matchapungo, Coree, Pamlico,and Bay River warriors joined with them. Prior to large-scale violence, an Englishman by the name of John Lawson had been captured during a surveying expedition up the Neues River. Along with Lawson were a German named Baron Christopher de Graffenried, two slaves (presumed to be African) and two native men. Lawson was responsible for a large sale of Tuscarora lands, which Baron de Graffenreid was the recipient. The Baron had plans to use the 17,500 - acre area to establish the town of New Bern. This sale was done with the Tuscaroras left totally out of the picture. This proved to be the act that was to trigger hostilities, as the Tuscaroras were now at the breaking point. When the opportunity presented itself to capture Lawson, it was seized upon. Taken through several villages, the captives were tried for actions that had been taken against the Tuscaroras. During the proceedings, which included chiefs from other communities, Lawson argued strongly in his favor and initially won the release of his party. Yet the morning after, while waiting on a means of transportation out of the area, Lawson got into a heated argument with the chief from the town of Cartuca, apparently threatening to take revenge on the Tuscarora people for this incident. With this, the party once again found themselves captive. A council condemned Lawson to death, but let the others go free. But this was not to happen until a war party returned to this town. His captors told de Graffenreid that they (the Tuscaroras) were to make war on the whites for all of the misdeeds that they had suffered. And while he certainly did not approve of his own captivity, and the war that was to take place against the (white) settlements, de Graffenfreid was to state later that he had for the most part been treated fairly while among the Tuscaroras, and acknowledged that many injustices had been perpetrated against them. He said of the Tuscaroras, "They seldom offend Christians without some motive for it, and the greatest part of the time, the abuse comes from the Christians, who deal roughly with them". One of the enslaved Africans was never seen again, believed to have run off to take his chances as far from white society as he could. The other, along with de Graffenreid made their way back to New Bern.

The result was the mobilization of large numbers of soldiers from the colonies of North and South Carolina. This not only served as a military operation, it turned the endeavor into a large-scale slaving expedition as more captives were taken to Charleston, South Carolina. From there, they were destined for locations in the Caribbean to suffer enslavement. There were warriors from native communities who joined in the efforts against the Tuscaroras, such as the Yamasees, Catawbas, Pedees, Watterees, Saxapaws, and the Essaws. By 1713, the war against the Tuscaroras reached a point that many decided to migrate north. As they were of Iroquoian descent they sought refuge with their relations that were prominent in parts of what is now Pennsylvania, New York, and southern Canada. In 1722, they became the sixth nation of the Haudenosaunee, the People of the Long House. Those who remained in North Carolina were now a fragment of what they had formerly represented. Sovereignty was now a thing of the past. Some of these enemies of the Tuscaroras were to find out that their breaking points were to come sooner than later. By 1715, most of the nations along the coastal areas from North Carolina southward had finally tired of their exploitation by the English. A census conducted during this time estimated that there was a combined total of 10,000 native people in the area of South Carolina-Georgia. These were numbers that commanded respect. The Yamasees finally rose up in April of 1715 when a delegation of representatives of Carolina Governor Charles Craven arrived at the Yamasee town of Pocotaligo. These delegates were killed, and Yamasee warriors began to attack English Farms in the countryside. The Yamasees were allied with Creeks from the lower towns (towns located near white settlements) as well as Apalachees. Many Creeks had become equally frustrated with the exploitive ways of the English who at one time they had also been allied. After a force of Carolina militia and native allies counterattacked the Yamasees, driving them southward below the Savannah River, some Yamasees, Creeks, and Apalachees were to migrate into northern Florida, as the Spanish who were located in and around Saint Augustine welcomed them because they (the warriors) were a thorn in the side of their mutual enemy, the English colonists of the Carolinas. These warriors in turn would come in contact with blacks who had taken refuge in Saint Augustine, and in turn, become warriors themselves. Many of these men were escaped slaves from the Carolinas who had succeeded in arriving in Saint Augustine. Having better prospects of a dignified life, these were willing and ready to fight against the English. Governor Craven added enslaved Africans to the militia ranks. Craven was also aware of tensions between Cherokees and Creeks, a fact he was to attempt to exploit to the advantage of the Carolinas. A representative from the Cherokee town of Echota arrived in Charleston South Carolina, to negotiate an alliance. Craven was to find out as would other whites who would attempt to forge pacts with other native nations that one representative did not represent the people in their entirety. No matter that there was cultural cohesion among a group of people who may occupy settlements over a vast area, political autonomy was a fact of life. So while an agreement was worked out with Echota, Craven was under the impression that he could expect aid from any Cherokee town. When Cherokee warriors didn't show up at a rendezvous with Colonial militiamen, Craven ordered a Colonel Maurice Moore to proceed to the Cherokee town of Tugaloo to find out what was going on. In Moore's command of three hundred militia were a number of armed black troops, as well as white ones. The Yamasee of South Carolina, various Cherokee and Chickasaw towns (among others) found themselves at different time under attack by black troops armed and directed by white commanders.

This was a pattern that would continue into the early twentieth century as various units of the United States Army, the 24th and 25th Infantry, 9th and 10th Cavalry, and the Seminole Negro Indian Scouts, (some of whom had native ancestry as well), would be used primarily against indigenous peoples of the northern and southern plains. This phenomenon was not restricted to men of African descent. Crow, Apache, Caddo, Delaware, and other native men were to become scouts for the United States military machine, leading these units against other native communities. In a twist of fate, around 1637, the Dutch, who were vying for control of Brazil, would use Tupi and Tapuya Warriors from Brazil on the Gold Coast of Africa to combat African peoples who were fighting against any number of European countries seeking to exploit a respective area. When Portugal finally established control of Brazil in 1654, those surviving Tupi and Tapuya were now in the position of spending the remainder of their lives in Africa, unless they could find a way back into Brazil undetected. The Portuguese were not about to welcome any allies of an enemy they had fought hard to dislodge from a contested area. Thus, some of these natives of the land that was to be known as Brazil never saw their homelands again.

Colonial authorities would often circulate stories throughout slave quarters as well as native communities, falsifying information to instill hostility and fear so the climate would at least be one of suspicion. Sometimes if an epidemic had recently descended on an indigenous community, Europeans made it a point to accuse Africans of being the source of the disease. These types of tactics would fan the flames of animosity between red and black. Throughout the east coast, Europeans would hire native warriors to hunt down their missing "property". Examining South Carolina is to see irony in the making. Natives who had been Christianized and designated "Settlement Indians" would often be used to hunt down and terrorize runaway slaves. It was in South Carolina that survivors of cultures such as the Peedee, Yuchi, Sara, and Cape Fear (among others) had found themselves uprooted due to differing forms of white encroachment, and became impoverished refugees living in camps near white towns. The effects of the encroachment varied from the taking of territory, to enslavement. The men of these nations would perform services for white settlers such as hunting run-aways. These escapees were of African or native ancestry, or a combination of the two (in some instances those being hunted were white indentured servants who would try to escape their terms of service). It had been in Florida where Christianized Natives had themselves been the victims of similar tactics inflict-ed on them from slave raids. Interestingly enough the decline (somewhat) of the enslavement of Native Americans can be attributed in part to the European fear of the possibility of potential alliances between red and black. It seems that when indigenous people who had been enslaved made their escape, they would often leave in the company of black comrades. There were reports of former slaves returning to liberate enslaved Africans who could not make the initial escape. Some of these circumstances were relatives returning to rescue loved ones. These groups of people would sometimes form their own communities while keeping a vigil against threats that were always present in the form of mercenaries, and slave catchers who could come in the form of native warrior, armed African slaves, as well as (white) military or civilian troops. As time passed it was appar-ent to the colonizing authorities that it was somewhat more profitable to traffic in Africans. The trafficking of Native Americans into slavery would decline, but not disappear entirely.

Native people who were found near the coast as well as inland at the time of European colonization included the Tutelo, Saponi, Occaneechee, Saura, Keyawee, Eno, Saxapahaw, Catawba, and Cherokee, one of the most numerous and powerful of the time. Primarily (but not exclusively) in the highland and mountain regions, at their peak, the Cherokee were spread out from Virginia, Tennessee, North Carolina, South Carolina, Georgia and Alabama. By the late 1830s, the removal process was accelerated as large numbers of Cherokees were forced out of North Carolina. Those who survived the Trail of Tears were to start new lives in the area designated "Indian Territory", eventually to be called Oklahoma. Here, they joined some of their relations who had already relocated there by choice some years prior. This was to lead to social upheaval that had its roots back in their respective homelands of the East. Some who stayed behind either went into exile in the most remote regions they could find, or assimilated into other communities while keeping their identities concealed, to be revealed only to the most trusted of loved ones.

In 1836, North Carolina passed a law declaring there were "Free People of Color". This category included those of African descent who were technically free, although anyone who had any degree of melanin content in their skin real-ized that freedom under those circumstances was at best precarious. There were those of native descent, but as far as the law was concerned, there were no more Indians, especially none who were recognized as being part of any sovereign enti-ty. Native people that still could be recognized as a distinct community posed a threat to the situation that was created to benefit white society (there was still a sizable Cherokee presence in western North Carolina). Thus, it was ever more important to get rid of any large, identifiable concentrations of native people. This scenario was hardly unique, as other states were to enact similar legislation that led to the paper extinction of a number of peoples. This in turn further opened the doors of the exploitation of the resources that were originally part of the lives of indigenous people. Yet with the possible mindset, however dominant or sublime, that red and black peoples were to be kept apart, led to the prosecution of couples that were categorized as being "unlawfully married". This charge carried the legal weight of being a felony. North Carolina State legal documents record that there were at least ten cases brought forth in the courts of Hyde County during 1843 that came under prosecution. These particular cases stated the defendants were living or cohabiting with slaves. This represented a situation that was "against the peace and dignity of the state". The names of some of these defendants were those who were of native descent, yet in the eyes of the law, they were "Free People of Color". No doubt, these marriages were brought to a tragic end. Apparently, there are times when love doesn't conquer all, especially when it represents to whatever degree a threat to a status quo (the white perspective of the time) that wants to maintain and enforce a specific type of social order.

But this type of persecution was certainly nothing new. Similar measures had been implemented prior to this time period and would be done so after the period as well. The British had imposed legal measures against the Montaukett people in the East Hampton area of Eastern Long Island (New York). Montaukett women that married men of African descent, or "foreign Indians" (non Montaukett), were subject to arrest. These laws existed well into the 20th century, as governments still enforced laws that forbade marriage to anyone outside of the immediate "tribe". In other words, if a Canadian Chippewa woman wished to marry a Lenape man that lived in the United States, she risked being expelled from the tribal rolls. The laws of the region also declared that children of such unions would have no rights in any land claims in the area. Because it was the norm to classify people of African descent, native descent, and any combination thereof as "colored" in what were originally colonies and later states, it is easy to overlook the fact that there was this type of diversity that was happening in many areas. Data taken in what is now northeastern Connecticut indicates that there was a percentage of families and individuals of "color" living in this region for a long period of time. This spanned a period of centuries. This is not a unique phenomenon. In native social structures, it was not unusual to adopt outsiders into a respective community. This had been occurring for centuries (as well). Community members were lost due to disease, warfare, or the accidents that sometimes happened. These individuals were replaced as circumstances allowed. These replacements were not always of indigenous origin, especially after 1492. In the east, and later in Oklahoma, as well as more western locales, there were families, and in turn, communities that could include among their ranks those that originally came from elsewhere.

Some Native Americans hunted and captured or sometimes killed runaway slaves (although escaped slaves were not always of African descent). Africans who had been enslaved were used to attack Native American communities. Monk Estil, a man of African descent gained notoriety as an "Indian fighter" in Kentucky during the 1770s . The Chuwasha of Louisiana came under attack in 1730 in the vicinity of New Orleans. The series of events that led to this attack grew out of the apprehensions of Governor Perier of French Louisiana. By 1728, runaway slaves of various complexions and ancestries had begun assembling throughout the territory, including New Orleans. This fed French fears, as it became clear that escaped Africans and native peoples (free and enslaved) had been unifying throughout the region. Maroon settlements began to dot the landscape along the woods and cypress swamps for miles. It was becoming a common occurrence for escaping Africans and natives to come together. Also, nations such as the Natchez, Chickasaws, and factions of the Choctaws had also begun to shelter Africans. These nations had many competent warriors and were forces to be respected for their prowess in combat. Having experienced some revolts as well as hearing reports of maroon raids on plantations, the French under the command of Perier began to devise tactics to drive permanent wedges between Africans and the indigenous population. The Chuwasha were diminished after the attack by enslaved Africans, although the survivors were believed to have relocated elsewhere. The stronger nations of the region, that is the Natchez, Choctaw, and Chickasaw, were approached by colonial representatives and asked to arrest and/or report to the French information about the escapees. This latter French action had limited success. On November 28,1729, Natchez warriors with the aid of African allies attacked and destroyed a French settlement coincidently named Natchez. When the French and some Choctaw allies counterattacked on January 27, 1730, they fought against a multi racial contingent of warriors comprised of Africans and Natchez. In spite of these French policies, Africans who had lived among the Natchez were only good for execution when back among the French, and those who had been among the Choctaw, as well as other nations in the area, were at best headaches for their (re) enslavers.

This was not the only instance of Governor Perier turning his attention to the issue of red-black alliance. New Orleans at this point in time, shared similar circumstances with other Euro- controlled urban areas and nearby surrounding regions of the time period. There was a considerable presence of enslaved native people. New York, Charleston, Boston, and other locales also laid testimony to this fact. Some were victims of war. Others the victims of outright kidnapping with the goal of supplying humans for the purpose of exploiting their lives to answer whatever lust for greed that came from capitalizing on available resources (i.e. the land and its bounties). From the ranks of the Chitimacha, Alibamon,and Taensa, came victims destined for suffering the fate. Many of these unfortunates were women. As typical of the pattern of the day most native men, if kept alive usually were shipped to slavery in the Caribbean. Those women who did not end up as mistresses to French slaveowners were destined to be partnered with enslaved African men. In 1727, a maroon village, known as Natanapalle, was discovered. There was a paranoia that struck at the heart of slaveholders everywhere of the uniting of these groups of people. This armed settlement (as it was wise for any maroon village to be) was a mixed community of red and black. The governor called for an end to the enslavement of native people. Altruism and love of humanity had nothing to do with his desire. The population of Africans in Louisiana was rapidly outgrowing the number of French. Those native slaves stood a better chance of escaping, and there was the real possibility that they would be accompanied by their African counterparts. By this time, these counterparts were not only fellow victims of the slave system; they were family. Governor Perier expressed his concern that Indian slaves mixing with enslaved Africans may cause them to desert in each others company, which had already happened in some instances. These relationships Perier feared would be disastrous for the colony when there were more blacks. The threat imposed by maroon settlements in Louisiana was to continue well into the mid 1800's. In 1861 there were reports of maroon settlements that alarmed the white aristocracy in particular throughout the state, as the early years of the civil war gathered momentum. What is of interest is that in some of these reports, there was mention of whites now residing in some of these settlements.

It wasn't only the possibility of red-black alliances that worried the French authorities of the region. Conditions were so bad that some soldiers sought out other means of survival. Low pay (and sometimes no pay), harassment and abuse from officers, bad food, and environmental conditions that often led to disease made some of these troops think about alternatives. There were reports of slaves (regardless of complexion) and indigenous people aiding disgruntled soldiers escape to native settlements, or Spanish Territories of Florida, Cuba, and what is now New Mexico. To prevent this cooperation, the French colonial officials used an old tactic; it was not unusual to have soldiers who had been convicted of an offense to be punished by either indigenous people or Africans. Given this reality, along with the fact that the primary responsibility of the soldiers to begin with was that of being used against the former, the stage was set for the familiar situation of divide and conquer. Certainly, this reality could hinder the thought of possible multiracial cooperation that would prove detrimental to the colony. As in other parts of the hemisphere the colonial authorities didn't hesitate to play off people against each other. native people hunting escaped slaves, and armed slaves raiding native and maroon settlements were situations that were common.

For those who had the misfortune of being kidnapped and forced into enslavement, this predicament didn't mean they had left everything behind. Those who were in control sought to exploit all possibilities from their enslaved victims. Some of the skills learned in Africa were to initially prove useful. Those who had familiarity with a tropical environment were able to adapt to the semi-tropical environment of what is now known as the southeastern United States (and certainly more so the Caribbean, Central, and some regions of South America). For those that had utilized riverine skills in the waterways of West Africa, these same skills would take these men into the hinterlands of the region. Similarly, in the French colonies of the lower Mississippi region, some enslaved Africans were used as rowers in areas that were sites of various native settlements. Upon doing so, these men became familiar with the vast system of water-ways that were characteristic of the region, as well as the surrounding land-scapes. The fact that these men were also coming into contact with the indige-nous peoples living in their respective areas was to lead these men to acquire some knowledge and understanding of the respective culture, protocols and cus-toms of a given area.

This knowledge could prove useful for those who were desperate and daring enough to attempt escape. By the 1780s, some of the bayous and adjacent water-ways approaching New Orleans were in the control of several maroon commu-nities, two of which were known by the names of Ville Gaillarde and Chef Menteur. It was also common knowledge that because of numerous settlements located between the mouth of the Mississippi River and New Orleans, maroons had the upper hand in this region as well. Certainly, the inhabitants of these set-tlements operating under martial conditions would have been predominately African. Yet there were not only Africans residing here, but indigenous people as well as any combination of racial mixtures. This was happening as many native communities east of the Mississippi River had begun to take on multi racial char-acteristics as intermarriages occurred.

While many communities remained distinctly indigenous, the possibility of intermarriage would increasingly be used against these communities wherever it was to the political/economic advantage of colonizing entities to exploit this sit-uation. This continues to be the case as the twenty-first century progresses. No doubt, native communities that had little or no intermarriage would come under attack as well. All of these settlements would be (and are) targets of those that would profit from their demise. From the 1500s into the 1900s and even 2000s (although now the tactics differ), indigenous communities would be alert for the approach of enemies, whatever their complexion. During the early years of the 1700s, in French colonial areas, the authorities were faced with the same situa-tion as some soldiers and settlers had intimate relations with African and indige-nous women. This happened in a variety of circumstances as in other parts of the hemisphere, some abusive, some consensual. It was felt that the offspring of such unions would only prove detrimental to the colony as a whole. Officially, this was not approved, but it was a fact. After 1717, with the increase in the number of European women rising, this was to decrease interracial encounters (that is, between white men and women of color), but it never stopped altogether.

Uprisings are hardly a new or unique phenomenon. They occur when oppressed people get fed up with their lot. Given the establishment of maroon societies throughout the western hemisphere, this was certainly no surprise, either. But when an army of enslaved and free people of African descent fought and established the nation of Haiti, the effect was frightening to those who had a stake in maintaining power and empowering to those oppressed people who received word of the revolt through a number of sources. This island, also known as Quisqueya, once witnessed the triumph of a group of Tainos who managed to fight for their chance of freedom in their own land under the leadership of Guarocuya (Enriquillo). Once suffering the indignity of slavery, these freedom fighters fled into the mountains, and after a prolonged guerilla war of self-defense, was approached by Spain who sued the people for peace. They would settle near the Cibao area of the island. This, the same island that was once home to such Taino leaders such as Coanabo, Guanagacari, and Anacaona, all of whom along with their people fell victim to treachery stemming from Spanish expansionism. Refugees from Haiti began to arrive on the continental mainland of North America. New Orleans, in particular had a long history of interaction with this specific island in the Caribbean. France had succeeded in colonizing both areas. The military and administrative skills of Toussaint Loverture frightened slaveholders of the island. The accomplishment of his military forces became definite grounds (for many) to escape from the island. What was started by Toussaint Loverture would be finished (after Loverture's capture and exile) by Henri Christophe. One destination was one where, at another point in time was a destination for commerce as well as rest and relaxation. This was the southern city at the mouth of the Mississippi River, New Orleans. Whites, as well as people with varying hues of skin color that accompanied them, spread the word of events happening on that island in the Caribbean. Another source of information came through sailors who were crewmen on ships that sailed between the United States and the islands of the Caribbean. With all its hazards, the sea was one of the options open to men, and men of color who were willing to take the risks involved with a maritime lifestyle. In the case of some men who could trace their ancestry to indigenous coastal cultures along the Atlantic, this was a way to continue a tradition, albeit altered to varying degrees. Some of these men, no doubt, were from cultures that had seen African intermarriage. Pequot, and Wampanoag cultures are only a few that had strong ties to the sea. Fishing and the hunting of sea mammals were part of their maritime heritage. With the decline of their respective societies, survival strategies took on a different meaning. Those men of African descent, regardless of other bloodlines, also looked to the sea. It became a fact that maritime ventures based out of the northeastern United States increasingly utilized a labor force that was increasingly, though not exclusively dark-skinned. In the face of bleak economic prospects in communities that had declined and, in some instances, ceased to exist, indigenous men that had lived in coastal communities and knew the ways of the sea looked for work from white employers. Some escaped slaves thought it was better to take their chances of survival, facing the wrath of an injured whale, rather than facing slavery. There were whalers who were of native descent, African descent, and a combination of both. In some instances, going to sea was a path of some mobility, as racial oppression continued to spiral on land.

Paul Cuffee, a man of African-Wampanoag ancestry, was a prominent sea captain in the late 1700s and early 1800s. During his career, Captain Cuffee would make several voyages to Africa. While there were a few captains of African descent commanding their own vessels, this industry in its different incarnations was white-controlled (another man of African-Wampanoag ancestry who was a mariner had already made his mark on history, Crispus Attucks, who was born in the "Praying Town" of Natick in Southern Massachusetts).

While there have been exceptions recorded about life at sea, along with this fact of white domination came the reality of racism that prevailed on shore. Some men of color, regardless of ancestry were enslaved, others were free. Yet there were many hazards in life at sea and the different ports of call where these ships docked. Laws were passed in southern cities with coastal ports, calling for the immediate imprisonment of anyone of African descent. Sailors of color were at risk just by being under the influence of their bodies' melanin content. There was the constant threat of being kidnapped into slavery; in the case of those sailors already enslaved, this was an issue of owners changing via kidnapping or sale to a different person. The sailor had nothing to do with this type of action other than being victimized. Being a victim of circumstance certainly had negative implication. South Carolina increasingly watched the population of people of color, and African descendants in particular, whether enslaved or free, surpassed the number of whites residing in the state. It was reported that an white immigrant to South Carolina said in 1737 that South Carolina had more "negroes" than white people within its borders. A census taken in 1724 indicated that there were fourteen-thousand whites, and thirty two-thousand "negroes" (both enslaved and free). The legislature in 1800 enacted a law in the effort to curtail the growth phenomenon. Under this law, the entry of any free "negro" or slave or servant of color, who had been brought in for the purpose of sale was prohibited. Any free person who was found guilty by jury of entering or being brought into the state was to be sold into slavery. Those individuals who assisted in the capture of the person who had entered the state were given a financial reward. Sailors were no exception from this policy and were at risk if the port of call was anywhere within the boundaries of South Carolina.

Haiti however offered citizenship to any sailor of African descent who arrived at its shores. Some sailors jumped at the chance, creating a diplomatic headache for ship captains and the United States Government, in particular. Technically, these men were citizens of the United States. The fact that some were enslaved and had no liberty, and those who were free had little rights to speak of, heightened the absurdity of the situation. Here was the opportunity to participate in a black nation of the western hemisphere. There were reports of some sailors who wanted asylum and citizenship but were barred from setting foot on Haitian soil, being escorted off ships under the protection of Haitian soldiers. White fleet owners and ship captains faced the dilemma of losing crew members. It was through these sailors, who were certainly worldly in their own right that the word of the accomplishments on Haiti was spread. The slaveholding class in the southern United States such as Georgia, Alabama and South Carolina were especially fearful. By now, it was known that in the territory called Florida were settlements occupied by indigenous people, and free Africans who, in some instances were autonomous, and in other instances allied with indigenous hosts. There was some intermarriage happening. Compounding these anxieties, some of the inhabitants of these settlements had raided some plantations on the border, taking away people who had been enslaved to a new life in the communities to the south. No doubt, that were some plantation owners that had visions of a dark hued army coming north across the border to wreak whatever kind of mass havoc into their lives. This type of fear certainly wasn't new. There was a longstanding concern that Africans and Native Americans would form alliances that could threaten the stability of Eurocentric-based societies throughout the hemisphere. Alliances and resistance was taking place on smaller scales throughout the hemisphere, as it was realized that there was common ground on which the oppressed could unify. In the United States, the Treaty of Ghent (1790) with the Creek Confederacy had a provision stating that any runaway slaves were to be returned to their owners. This was only one of many divide and conquer tactics that were being implemented. With the establishment of the Republic of Haiti, paranoia was truly taking hold in the minds of some. Those who made a living from the capture and sale of human beings sometimes risked going after a human commodity in Florida. And while there were financial incentives that led to ventures into Florida, some of these efforts cost these hunters their lives. While some individuals and small groups no doubt fell victim to these insidious acts, large- scale endeavors were dangerous. The communities in Florida were armed and prepared to defend their residents. Once large scale operations began to take place in the peninsular, the soldiers, mercenaries, and the government that had hired them found this out time and time again. By the decline of hostilities in 1858, the lives of more than fifteen hundred U.S. Military personnel and fifty million dollars had been expended against the peoples now collectively known as Seminoles.

Ikanyusksa - the land blessed by the sun, the moon, and their children the stars, to be later known as Eecheebee (Deer Nose) by later native immigrants from Alabama and Georgia, was certainly inviting for a number of reasons. Called Florida by the Spanish, it was to play a crucial role in events that were to effect various groups of people. By the mid-1700s, the original population was decimated by disease and slave raids. The Appalachee, Timicua, Tequesta, Calusa, and smaller nations were hit hard by these bad circumstances. This land was the focal point of various European interests, as Spain, France, and England ping-ponged for control. During this time period, different factions of the Creek Confederacy began to make their way south to settle in territory that was once inhabited by some of the aforementioned nations. This confederacy was itself multi faceted, in that various groups of people speaking different languages comprised membership. The Yamasee War of 1715, and the King George War which ended in 1748, were only two factors that slowed the southern migration of people. Oconees, Appalachicolas, Miccosukees, Yamasee, Yuchi, Choctaws, Shawnees, Alabamus, Stonos, and Chiahas, were among the earliest to make the journey of resettlement. Linguistically, these groups for the most part spoke related but different languages. Some spoke Hitchiti, now commonly called Mikasuki. This survives today among some of the Seminole and Miccosukee people of Florida. Other migrations were to continue with the last major influx occurring after the Creek Civil War ended in 1814 (this was not to be the last instance of major civil upheaval among the Creeks that would escalate into bloodshed). Groups such as Tallasees were to be among the latter arrivals. These migrants spoke Muscogee, more commonly referred to as Creek. Spain and

England were the major players in the area, and the migrants, who had their own autonomous communities (contrary to what some Creeks wanted to think), were to play off these nations against each other. But these were not the only people traveling and settling in this area. Fisherman out of Cuba fished the waters off Florida and, in some instances would settle for periods of time on the peninsula. Given the intermixing of bloodlines happening throughout the Caribbean, it is an educated guess that some of these fishermen had indigenous as well as African blood. Some of these fishermen intermarried with women from the indigenous communities, and fathered children by them.

The Spanish, in order to be a thorn in the side of the British, spread the word that any escaped slave would be welcomed in Florida. As early as 1687, enslaved people living in British territories of the southeast began to take their chances by fleeing south. British territorial possessions at the time included North and South Carolina, Virginia, parts of Georgia, Pensacola in Western Florida, and Mobile, Alabama. The enslaved people of the southeast were of African descent, some were indigenous descent, and/or a combination of the two.

Florida was a beacon to those who were willing to make the dangerous journey southward. Perils such as slave catchers were real. A captured runaway was in a terrible position, as the punishments for the captured were brutal. The government of South Carolina instituted monetary rewards for the capture of runaways, dead or alive. This incentive led to white men in particular, and some native men into the occupation of hunting people. Mutilation played a role in this system of rewards. Bounties for scalps and the number of ears brought back would be rewarded financially. Any runaway also had to deal with natural hazards. Traveling established roads and paths frequented by the general population was certainly not the best option for those seeking to escape. This meant traversing through areas that were still in a natural state. The southern wilderness presented its own formidable challenges in terms of environmental barriers as well as threats from animal species, be they insect, reptilian, and/or mammalian. For those that managed to journey by sea, the maritime environment posed its own set of hazards. Yet many risked all, for the prize was great indeed: Freedom.

The Spanish settlement of Saint Augustine witnessed over time an influx of these refugees who had taken the risks in making the exodus from wince they came. In return for refuge, the Spanish asked that the refugees make themselves available for the defense of the territory. Given the conditions from which many had escaped. they were more than willing and ready to comply with this request. In 1737, The Spanish built a stronghold for these refugees to be known as Fort Mose. The warriors of this fort were paid as Spanish soldiers and were commanded by officers from within their own ranks. By the time of the British invasion of 1740, under the command of James Oglethorpe of Georgia, these warriors, along with allies from local indigenous communities, were ready to combat the invaders. A Spanish counterattack into Georgia during June 1742 saw black soldiers participating in combat, as these soldiers were now defending what was their new homeland. Over time some of these warriors would intermarry with women from nearby indigenous communities. Spain would briefly cede Florida to the British in 1763. Yet escaped slaves continued to travel into Florida and establish or move into existing settlements. Sometimes these settlements would become affiliated with local indigenous communities. Given the phenomenon taking place in northern Florida of the influx and settling of former Creeks and other indigenous people(s), as well as Africans (some of whom were formerly enslaved), the framework was set on the establishment of what would eventually be called Seminole communities. By the 1790s, events on an island in the Caribbean (Haiti) sent shock waves through the slaveholding classes and white supremists in general. By the turn of the 1800s the ruling class in the southeastern United States were quite fearful as to what they believed was happening in Florida. There was some slaving activity happening. This was not a new phenomenon. In prior centuries, native peoples of the peninsula were victims of raids that came from the north, as well as various marine points. These communities at the time had been weakened by disease, and the fact was that many had converted to Christianity and moved to missions that had been established by Catholic priests. In military terms, these establishments were poorly armed, if at all. The combination of these events was devastating. What was distinct was that by the early 1800s these communities were capable of defending themselves from outside threats, such as slave raids. Many warriors of these territories were well armed.

In some instances, they had firearms obtained from either the British, Spanish, or even both. Other forms of weaponry, such as the bow was also prevalent. Certainly in the hands of one that is versed in its use, weaponry of any kind commands respect. Some reports came back into Georgia and South Carolina that the black settlements were known to have men drilling under the supervision of their own commanders. Some of these communities were allied with nearby native settlements. There had also been numerous instances that further played upon the fears of the southern aristocracy and a growing number of American settlers who were now occupying areas of Spanish Florida. This group in particular was becoming more vocal about what should happen to Florida, i.e., change hands and become a part of the United States. Escaping slaves continued heading south into Florida. By the beginning of the early 1810s, there was an increase in clashes between whites on the Georgia-Florida border, and warriors who were of African descent, native, or of mixed bloodlines who were residents of the peninsula to the south. These skirmishes kept increasing and served as a prelude to what was to happen on a larger scale, escalating in 1817, 1835, and 1855 when regular military units, mercenaries, and volunteers met in combat against people who were to be called Seminoles. These entities would, time and time again in this period prove to be ready to deal with any infringement that threatened their homes and loved ones. Small-scale engagements occurred into the teens. After the conclusion of the War of 1812, General Andrew Jackson, after a diversion in fighting with and against factions of the Creek Confederacy, focused on the "Spanish" territory of Florida. This man certainly represented a type of disposition characterized by the upper society of the old south. He was a slaveholder and had a stake in the slave trade (even though technically, the importation of kidnapped victims had been outlawed in 1807). Jackson was a master manipulator, and he had proven on other occasions how cunning he could be in many instances. He certainly knew how to fan the flames of animosity among the Creek Confederacy. And Jackson, along with white troops, some "progressive" Cherokees, as well as some Creeks opposed to their own brethren, fought in the Creek Civil War of 1813-14. This culminated at the Battle of Horseshoe Bend, where several hundred Red Stick Warriors would lose their lives. The name of Andrew Jackson would come to be reviled by many native peoples of the southeast. During the Viet Nam War, The Nixon Administration ordered the U.S. Military to take covert actions into Laos. Once this became known to the general public, the outrage led to massive protests throughout the country. But this type of action was nothing new. In July of 1816, Andrew Jackson ordered ground and naval units to lay siege to a location that had become known as the "Negro Fort". This site was located at Prospect Bluff on the Appalachicola River in northwestern Florida. This well- armed abandoned British fort had been taken over primarily, but not exclusively, by blacks. This was an irritant for the slaveholding class of Alabama and Georgia. It was also felt that any American seacraft sailing up the Appalachicola River attempting to trav- el with cargo to locations on the Chattahoocheks and Flint Rivers (which had links with the Appalachicola) were in danger from bombardment from the Negro Fort. The fort was directly located on the travel route. The commander of the fort, known as Garcon, gave good reason for the sense of paranoia. This site became a stronghold, and from here, settlements rose up in the immediate vicinity. The residents were confident that they were protected from harm due to the proxim- ity to the fort. Armed warriors based at the fort reinforced this sense of security. Jackson ordered a ground and naval force under the command of General Duncan Clinch to lay siege to the fort. The ground force, consisting of U.S. Army troops and some Creeks friendly to America, traveled southward overland toward the fort, while the naval force traveled upriver from the Gulf of Mexico. After a four day bombardment, a shell from one of the naval vessels hit the magazine stores of the fort, setting off a massive explosion. This provided the opening for the ground force to breech what was left of the fort. Garcon and a Choctaw man were captured alive, tortured, then executed. Some residents of the area found themselves kidnapped victims, bound for the slave markets of Alabama and Georgia. But for those who escaped, word spread to other settlements that the things were escalating. Although this act had been taken without presidential or congressional authorization, Jackson would be rewarded by the government at a later time. Jackson would eventually exploit those native peoples who had been allies. He was to set in motion events that would lead to the Trail of Tears for southeastern, as well as other eastern peoples who were to be exiled to Indian Territory. And the welfare and safety of the people was not a priority. At the end of this hostility that was the Creek Civil War (one of several conflicts that was to take place over an eighty-year period), there would be a migration of refugees heading south into Florida that would swell the ranks of the existing communi- ties. These refugees represented a spectrum of Creek culture, spanning racial bloodlines. Among these refugees was a young boy, traveling with his family. This particular group were of the Tallassees, whose original home was in Alabama. The young boy one day would grow up to be the great Seminole patriot, Osceola.

The destruction of the Negro Fort was only one step in the drama escalating in northern Florida. Other settlements stood in the path of combined forces consisting of white U.S. Soldiers and some Creeks who thought it better to take their chances allying with the American Army (this attitude was not shared by all Creeks). Border skirmishes between Seminoles and whites continued. By August of 1817, Kenhadjo, chief of a Miccosukee band living near Lake Miccosukee in north Florida received a letter from General Gaines. It is reported that Gaines accused Kenhadjo of sheltering blacks, and that he (Gaines) intended on scouring the area in the attempt to find them. Kenhadjo sent a reply stating that he wasn't sheltering any blacks, and he warned Gaines not to trespass on the lands of his people. Ironically, Kenhadjo, up until this time, had not been involved with any hostilities toward whites. Fowl Town, located in Georgia near the Florida border, would come under similar threats from the U.S. Army. The chief of this town, Neamathla, had warned the Army to stay away from this village. The Army attacked in October and November (1817). With this attack things intensified further. Seminoles of varying complexions attacked white settlements and businesses (those sympathetic to the United States) all over the northern part of the peninsula. When Andrew Jackson took command by January of 1818, he made plans for his forces to attack the remaining known Seminole towns and any town or outpost sympathetic to them. That is, the few Spanish and British trading posts in the region. This included Saint Marks and Pensacola. By mid-April of 1818, Jackson's forces attacked the settlement of Bowlegs and adjacent black towns located on the Suwanee River. The warriors from these towns fought a delaying action while their families escaped. After the fall of the towns on the Suwanee River, some refugees re- established small camps in more isolated areas of the region, while others headed further south into the peninsular. While there were already some settlements in the region, several new towns would be established in the Tampa area. Spain ceded Florida to the United States in January 1819, setting the stage for the next major confrontation that was to come.

Regardless of the fact there were numerous Seminole towns still in North and Central Florida, white expansion began to grow all over the area. This led to a common ideology that was played out time and time again throughout the hemisphere. The Indians must go. What further fanned this sentiment of whites in Florida was the fact that there were black towns located there as well. Tensions continued to rise. By 1823 the Treaty of Camp Moultrie was signed by some chiefs, even though these men did not represent all of the bands of people. As far as whites were concerned, they (the chiefs) were responsible for all of the settlements and towns. This treaty gave a five million acre reservation to the "Seminoles". The government also made promises to distribute provisions and provide other services necessary for living. When the promises were kept, the results were at best, inadequate. No one among the chiefs was familiar with the area that was being given to them. As many lived in established settlements, they didn't have reason to explore this unknown area to the south. This land, located in the central portion of the state, was a swampland that was no good for any kind of sustainable agriculture. To make matters worse, hunting was equally as bad. This land was heavily infested with insects, and filled with water not suitable for drinking. The people were miserable. There were reports of death by starvation coming out of the reservation. This led to some Seminole men who were living on the reservation to steal what they could from white farms and towns located in more livable areas. And while the white authorities were well aware of the condition of the Seminoles living on the reservation (a state of dire poverty), their main concern was the fact that their livestock and farms were being preyed upon. Slavehunters victimized any black person they could get who strayed from the relative safety (in numbers) of the towns. Violence occurred with increasing regularity. As bad as this scenario was, things were about to get worse.

By 1825, plans were in the making to remove Seminoles out of Florida to a region called "Indian Territory". This area included much of present-day Oklahoma and parts of Arkansas. The plan began to gain momentum under the Monroe presidency. This plan was not a new one. Similar scenarios had already been envisioned for other southeastern peoples. To add insult to injury, the plan for the Seminoles called for them to be settled among the Creeks. As there was still animosity between the two, this was a plan bound for failure. By the time Andrew Jackson become President in 1828, the dye was firmly cast.

The Second Seminole War (1835-42) certainly took its toll on the people. A horrific price was paid. People tried as best they could regarding the observances of cultural occasions. There were reports of Green Corn ceremonies happening during the early years of hostilities. But war dictated its own realities. As the war progressed it became more difficult to properly observe protocols. Because of the nature of war, there would be no regularity regarding the observances of spiritual practices. There was the uncertainty of agricultural efforts that could be suddenly interrupted by enemy attack. The numerous bands of people lived with the reality that they were refugees seeking sanctuary in their own lands. The raising of children became all the more difficult. Care for the elderly was jeopardized. The same was for the conditions of the sick. These are only a few of the realities faced when living in a state of martial readiness. An accurate number of Seminole lives lost during the conflict may never be known, and there were the consequences that survivors endured as a result of the turmoil created during and in the aftermath of war. By the time of its conclusion in 1842, many had been removed to Indian Territory to face new trails and tribulations. Billy Bowlegs and his band were among the last Seminole people who were to be deported west. He and his band departed for Indian Territory from Fort Myers in May of 1858. Although fate had Billy Bowlegs dying from smallpox in the winter of 1863, he would fight on the side of the Union in the civil war, earning the rank of captain. There were some Seminoles who never left their sanctuaries in the vast reaches of the Florida interior, such as the Everglades, Big Cypress Swamp, and other areas of pinelands and sawgrass that for whatever reason were marginalized (at best) and/or undesirable for white habitation. These areas became the refuge for the family groups that hid out, avoided detection, and would enter a prolonged period of isolation lasting for decades.

In some ways, the civil war of 1861-1865 took further attention away from those now finding refuge deep in Central and Southern Florida interior. Military resources of the United States and the Confederate States of America had other priorities With which to concern themselves. Anyone hiding in the pine stands and the hammocks of the Everglades, dealing with the challenges of this wilderness environment, were the furthest thing from the minds of warring factions fighting elsewhere. While there was to be some intermittent contacts with whites who learned how to traverse (to whatever degree) the wilderness areas of Florida, the policy of isolation was necessary as a survival strategy.

These groups would capitalize on the resources of the land and continue to thrive as free people beholden to themselves and answering only to the laws of the natural environment. Although the hostilities that characterized the Third Seminole War ceased after 1858, there would continue to be reports of maroons throughout the peninsular who would surface to wreak havoc near white settlements up to and during the civil war, a phenomenon not unique to Florida, but found throughout the south. Information that came from areas such as Marianna and Tallahassee stated there were guerilla activities in the region. One of the results was the liberation of slaves, the fate of whom is difficult to trace. One can speculate as to whom and what the composition of these communities of maroons looked like.

There were different types of alliances. In some instances, there were strong community ties because of intermarriage. Other times, the alliance was one of common cause. In colonial New York during 1712, there was a fear of a planned uprising involving men of African descent with the aid of some of the local Algonquin men. In the aftermath of fires that occurred in lower Manhattan, sixteen enslaved men were executed by differing means, which included hanging, burning, starvation, and the wheel. This happened in spite of the fact that colonial authorities found no evidence of a conspiracy. A law was also passed, outlawing the carrying of firearms by any black or native person. A woman of African descent in alliance with several Shinnecock men were discovered in a conspiracy to set fire to buildings of a colonial official in Southhampton, New York, during 1656. During the brief Stono Uprising (1739) in South Carolina, as the group of escaping slaves headed south, rumors spread that they were to be met by a band of warriors from Florida, comprised of Africans and natives. In the wake of the incident at Stono, the government of South Carolina implemented further legislative measures that further assaulted the humanity of those of African descent, be they enslaved or free. These were passed in an atmosphere that had undertaken measures over the years to degrade and humiliate African descendants. Indigenous peoples were treated similarly, unless, for whatever reason a particular native nation was in alliance with the colonial government. The one question that was highlighted in the legislation passed in 1740 was that all"Negro, Indian, Mulatto, and Mestizo", were legally presumed to be a slave, and all of the aforementioned "are declared to be, and remain forever hereafter, absolute slaves". A report published during 1768 in the Boston Chronicle stated that a military contingent had engaged in combat maroons, who were "a collection of Mulattoes, Mustees (a term used to describe persons of African/Native American ancestry) and Free Negroes". In some colonies, not only was there a fear of red-black alliances, but of multiracial alliances that would include poor whites. These were usually those that were serving in the capacity of indentured servants. The ruling class in Virginia and South Carolina undertook measures to insure this would not happen. English colonists began to occupy the territory now known as Georgia in 1733. In this area were people such as the Savannahs, Yuchis, Apalachees, Appalachicolas, Yamasees, Tamalhi, Hitchiti, Oconee, Kawita, and Tuckabatchee. These are some of the Muskogean people who resided in what was known as the lower towns of the Creek Confederacy. Other people such as the Yamacraw and the Cherokee, resided in the region. There had been periods of hostility directed at the settlers of South Carolina (usually after provocation). This colony was looking for a buffer to absorb of the aggression that might have been focused on their settlements.

Poor whites were to fulfill this capacity in Georgia. Because of the large number of slaves, most of whose population was increasingly African, there were constant fears of uprisings. The colonists in Georgia were seen as a resource in the event of these kinds of incidents. The fear of red-black alliance haunted South Carolinians. In 1736, it was brought to the attention of James Oglethorpe, a colonial trustee who wielded considerable influence, that on a plantation near Ebenezer Georgia, were enslaved Africans. This plantation was in close proximity to a native town. Oglethorpe commanded that the Africans be sent away immediately. Ironically, when Georgia formally accepted slavery into its region it became more difficult to track runaway Africans. Prior to formal acceptance of slavery, there were few Africans in the area. This implied that anyone of African descent seen was likely to be an escapee (probably from South Carolina). Spotting runaways would now be more difficult. As fate would have it, there was to be white intermarriage over time with the Creeks and the Cherokees, as white men looked to make alliances for profit from business ventures. English, Irish, and Scottish surnames would eventually become common among the Creek and Cherokee populations. A result was that there was an increasing growth of people of these communities who shared indigenous and European ancestry. As years would progress, these mixed bloods began to sway the culture(s) toward a different worldview, part of which was the adopting of chattel slavery.

There were instances where other alliances took place. These scenarios were to be played out over a period spanning centuries. One can look at the multiracial coalition led by the Lumbee warrior Henry Berry Lowry who fought against oppression in the woods and swamps of North Carolina, covering a period from 1864 to 1874. Those who fought at the side of Lowry ran the gamut of the color spectrum. Many native peoples in North Carolina (those who hadn't been forced on the Trail of Tears or went into hiding in remote areas) had been legally designated "Free People of Color". Many would be coerced into positions of hard labor for the army of the Confederate States of America. Lowry's destainfor oppression had its roots in the circumstances of the civil war, as he and other Lumbees fought guerilla actions against confederate units operating in the Carolinas. The Lumbees, true to the proud tradition set forth by this distinguished ancestor, would drive out a faction of the Ku Klux Klan from Robeson County, North Carolina, in 1958. That year, members of the Klan had decided to hold a rally in the town of Maxton, where a large number of Lumbee people resided. Crosses had been burned recently at the homes of two Lumbee families. In this backdrop the stage was set for the descendants of Lowry to uphold the legacy of their heritage. It is said that more than three hundred armed Lumbees showed up at the Klan rally. After a gun was fired into the air, some of the greatly outnumbered Klansmen were disrobed, disarmed (these weapons were given to the police after the event) and run out of the county. Another multiracial coalition of culturally conservative Seminoles, Creeks, African Americans, and poor whites would stand up to injustices in Oklahoma during 1917 in the Green Corn Rebellion. In Indian Territory, many lawmen went on the hunt for outlawed gangs of various ancestries. There were reports that roaming bands of Comanche in Texas had black compatriots among their ranks. One of the most notable was a bugler who participated in the siege of Adobe Walls, a small settlement located in northern Texas that catered to white buffalo hunters in 1874. An earlier report of 1851 was chronicled in the Houston Telegraph. This report stated that more than fifteen hundred escaped American slaves were allied with Comanche bands in Mexico and assisting these bands as allies in raids. Slavehunters venturing into Mexico found they would get more than they bargained for. Not only was the existence of these warriors in compliance with Comanches present, but there were now communities of Seminoles residing in some areas of northeast Mexico. Some of the men in these communities had firsthand experience in dealing with the kind of threat that the attempts of roaming slavehunters posed. The legacy left behind in Florida was a testimony to the fighting prowess and determination of these communities that would not hesitate to defend themselves. One would think twice at the possibility of an encounter that was a threat to either Seminoles or Comanche if one valued the thought of a long life. A cowboy named Nat Love, who became known in some circles as Deadwood Dick, said he was once captured by warriors of "Yellow Dog's Band". He would say after his escape that possibly one reason of how he gained the trust of the band was because there was a large percentage of "colored blood" among them.

In more contemporary times, the possibility of economic ties may have been a cause of concern in some circles. In 1977, a coalition of indigenous nations in the southwestern United States attempted to obtain federal and private sector funds in an attempt to initiate projects for reservation-centered businesses. The Council of Energy Resource Tribes comprised more than twenty nations. It was founded in 1975 with one of the goals of developing mineral resources in circumstances that would be favorable to its respective communities. Initially refused by the government, as well as the private sector, monies were finally obtained from both sources when stories began to circulate that the coalition, supposedly at the suggestion of then Navajo tribal chairman Peter MacDonald, had approached the Organization of Petroleum Exporting Countries (OPEC) with a similar proposal. At the time this was happening, the membership of OPEC consisted of the countries of Iran, Iraq, Kuwait, Saudi Arabia, Venezuela, Indonesia, Libya, The United Arab Emirates, Algeria, Nigeria, Equador, and Gabon. There had been a time before the invasion of the hemisphere when there had been trade networks that extended throughout the hemisphere. Trade items were interchanged, and through the network of trade, there was interaction with people in what is now Central and South America and people of the southwest, as well as other regions. If this union could have been achieved, one could only speculate to where this type of economic alliance would lead. Because of this, there was a change of heart on the behalf of funding sources located in the federal government of the United States, and monies were allocated for the consortium.

Sometimes there would not be incentives from Europeans to seek out runaways, and hunters would take after runaways on their own. Raiding was not a unique phenomenon and had occurred for any number of reasons, including slaving. For some warriors, the distinction of the pursued was of little importance in that there was an opportunity for (in some instances) honor, in addition to gain in terms of either money or items such as firearms and ammunition. At times the captives would be sold or ransomed back to the Europeans. There were other times however, when the captives would find themselves in the company of their captors for lengths of time (sometimes permanently). These conditions led to some interesting situations. In the 1700s Africans who had been captured by nations in the vicinity of New Orleans, such as the Chickasaws, found they had complete liberty in the Chickasaw community. These Africans would contribute to the welfare of the community by hunting. As time passed, some Chickasaws gained a reputation for being cruel to Africans. This would happen as some factions among the Chickasaws gained political power and were influenced by the negative elements of Eurocentric culture as the eighteenth and nineteenth centuries progressed. This theme would be prevalent time and time again among various nations, but for the sake of brevity the focus here is on what came to be designated the "Five Civilized Tribes". Over a period of time, there was intermarriage with whites that, for any number of reasons, would be spending great lengths of time within a specific community. This was certainly not unique as we look up and down the hemisphere, this happening with varying degrees of frequency. What began to happen in the southeastern United States was that as time went on, elements of Eurocentric culture would begin to influence aspects of life among a respective community. Again, this is hardly a new situation, as cultures throughout the world have influenced each other since the beginning(s) of humanity. In some situations, settlements be they indigenous or European, considered to be located on the frontier became multiracial centers of activity. Trading posts were usually established in these locations as colonial merchants took advantage of the new markets opening to them as they came in contact with various indigenous peoples, as well as non-native settlers, planting roots in a given area. Here in these backcountry locations, the process of mutual acculturation was in full swing. Increasingly, indigenous men could be seen wearing European shirts along with their leggings and moccasins. At the same time, many Europeans, and to an extent African men (who were not enslaved) adapted native-style dress in varying degrees, which was more appropriate for this kind of environment that was usually rural. Indigenous settlements became places where traditional housing structures had log cabins next to them. As native communities found themselves thrust into an economic situation that was global in proportions, the reliance on European goods became common. This happened to the degree that traditional tools and items of daily living were supplanted. Metal kettles, pots, pans, glass beads, sewing needles, axes, hoes, shovels, and rifles were among the many items that replaced objects common to native lifestyle(s). Some indigenous communities adopted African and European methods of farming. Similarly, Europeans and Africans came to rely on hunting, fishing and agricultural techniques used by native peoples. Healing methods known to indigenous people(s) were adopted by these new settlers in the (respective) area. There was a down side to all of this. Entrepreneurs who had established the economic venues in or near native communities didn't necessarily have the best interest of those communities in mind. In some instances, indigenous people who found their credit overextended for any reason time and time again witnessed their homelands shrinking as some white businessmen of (at best) questionable scruples tried to obtain land. As the demand for certain products such as deerskins increased as the local resources decreased, native hunters would increasingly venture further from traditional hunting grounds to different areas to hunt deer. This would cause conflicts with the peoples already using the resources of the area. Since the men were the best and the strongest of their communities, those communities were vulnerable in terms of raids from enemy forces of whatever complexion. Hard alcohol seemed to find its way into these communities. These beverages were usually a combination of rum or whiskey, mixed with any number of components that could be described as rotgut. The instances of substance abuse grew to the point of undermining the welfare of communities as some men and women succumbed to induced stupors. Similar trends have been witnessed into the twenty-first century in many urban inner city neighborhoods. It's not unusual to find certain economic interests based outside of a community establish venues within a neighborhood. Sometimes these big businesses don't feel they necessarily have a stake in terms of what's happening in the community, and it is, at times, only when there is pressure from those communities when those businesses put anything into the community as far as resources and services are concerned. These interests often overshadow and monopolize markets with which smaller businesses with roots in the community cannot compete. In the realm of substance abuse, hard drugs seem to always have a way of being readily available in spite of the "War on Drugs". Crack, heroin, etc., have become the rotgut substances of the time period.

With the increasing dependence on European goods, there were some individuals that saw the larger scenario and attempted to turn the tide. Tecumseh of the Shawnee was one such person. He traveled vast distances in the attempt of forming a continental alliance. He called for the return of self-sufficiency and for the reliance on resources and endeavors within the indigenous communities. Parallels can be drawn between this man and men such as Malcom X and Marcus Garvey. Although there are distinctions regarding the situations and solutions faced by Tecumseh and his contemporaries, there is common ground that can be found when listening to the messages of Garvey and Malcolm X. It can certainly be argued that the dependence on materials from outside of one's immediate cultural realm, especially to the point where these materials and the products they spawn take the place of objects specific to the culture, without the means to control the resources that create the materials, is the first step leading to economic domination. In contemporary times, those nations that are on the road to self sufficiency and autonomy are targeted for all types of backlash. But it is this concept of autonomy that has been advocated by those with insight on a regular basis over the centuries. The men mentioned are only a few examples of those who champion this status. The status of autonomy continues to play a pivotal role throughout the world, as conflicts ranging from the realm of economic sanctions to military incursion are utilized as the tug of war continues as nations jockey for positions that are in their respective interests. During his time, Tecumseh realized this, looking at the immediate situation as well as the larger picture. For those entities that sought (and seek) economic domination, there is no limit as to the tactics that could (and can) be implemented. The decline of the Plains people is one instance. With the decimation of the bison herds, the entire foundation of the numerous Plains cultures were hit hard. This animal was (is) the center of existence for many of these cultures. No part of the animal was wasted after a successful hunt. The flesh was used for food, and the bones, internal organs, and tendons were used for implements of various types. Many spiritual rituals evolved around the bison. With the decline in its numbers, government agencies and unscrupulous businessmen had many people of these nations at their mercy. Once the people were relocated by whatever means to reservations, they were, for the most part, dependent on whatever was provided for them. Except for instances where there were agency personnel at these locations who sought to treat the people fairly (most of the time, an exception, not the rule), most had to settle for inadequate provisions. And while the provisions were somewhat acceptable, they certainly were not as nutritionally sound as the diet that had been known prior to white expansion. Even where there had one time been the possibility of hunting other kinds of game in an effort to sustain family and community, these opportunities were far and few between. White expansion was having an environmental impact. During the early years, when the Plains people had been subjugated onto reservations, there were attempts by some of their relations to maintain their way of life. But when bison were found, they were few in number. The journey to find these animals became a daunting task as hunters had to range further and further in an effort to locate these animals. Alternative sources of game had also greatly diminished. In some instances, those hunters and family groups that traveled with them headed northward on their endeavors. This sometimes led to awkward diplomatic relations between the governments of the United States and Canada. The Hunkpapa under Sitting Bull is the most notable situation that occurred in the aftermath of Custer's defeat at the Greasy Grass (Little Bighorn) during 1876. He and his people remained in Canada until 1881, when they returned south to the United States and surrendered. Originally, when bands of native people traveled over vast areas, this scenario set the stage for interactions of various sorts between indigenous sovereign entities that historically ranged over these territories. If relations were good, agreements were reached that proved beneficial. There had been a history of conflict between some nations such as the Lakota and Blackfoot. White encroachment and domination on both sides of the 49th Parallel changed this picture entirely (the same can be said of the border with Mexico, although here, there was a record of armed conflict with the United States). To the government way of thinking, the possibility of having armed "Indians" with guns outside of the boundaries of the established reservations could readily lead to violent confrontation, regardless of the fact that by this point in time, many native people had put aside the thought of further armed resistance. Being at the mercy of the United States meant that autonomy was beyond the reach of the people. These communities were now in a position where they had to approach outsiders for their most basic needs of survival. With this being a fact, those who were calling the shots may or may not have the community's best interest at heart. When a nation is dependent on the another nation to provide for it, there is a distinct disadvantage for the nation that is in the position of having to wait on the response of the provider. Not being able to control one's destiny at best is detrimental.

As native communities in the east at one time seemed to be an alternative to those of African descent, free or enslaved, who were compelled to flee white societies, the plains and mountains of the west also beckoned. Any geographic location far from white settlements was a requisite. During the period of slavery in the United States, there were voices that spoke out in opposition to this horrible institution. The Abolition Movement played a role in a number of states to the elimination of slavery. Yet to be of African descent and be in any part of the United States was to have a life that was, at best, insecure. States that passed laws against slavery were often filled with contradiction, such as those passed in the Pennsylvania. Any person perceived to have African ancestry could instantaneously find themselves in any number of situations that could have devastating circumstances. In choosing to flee, one had to learn quickly to survive in a natural environment that could provide for life, but was also at once unforgiving to those who didn't have the ability to adapt. With the reality of this situation being a given, one was at least free as long as there was the will to survive, the strength to implement survival strategies, and white expansion kept at a distance. Many men (and after the civil war, in particular) and women struck out for the west to take their chances. Once this choice was made, life in the east was no longer a viable option. In the period of the early 1800s, men looking to leave behind the "norms" of society took their chances in this vast region. In the minds of many, to take one's chances with the possibility of starvation, dehydration, frostbite, all manners of animal attack, and disease was preferable to the climate and conditions perpetrated by a society steeped in racist viewpoints of varying degrees and intensities. With the expansion of the fur trade into vast regions of the west, in particular, the Rocky Mountains, there was work to be found if one had the willpower and physical strength to rise to the occasion. Working in this environment presented situations that were unforgiving to those who could not meet its terms of survival. And this was prevalent on a yearlong basis, as each season brought forth its own set of hazards of which to be aware of.

In the environment that spanned the northern and southern plains, the mountains and the western coastal areas there would be contact with different nations, such as the Absaroka (Crow), the Blackfoot Confederation, Flathead, Lakota, Mandans, Nez Perce, Shoshone, Apache, Comanche, Bannock, Ute, Paiute, Cheyenne, Arapaho, Dine (Navaho), Kootenay, and Kiowa, as well as many others. These various groups of people were maintaining ways of living that were on the verge of monumental changes, and not for the better. Many nations of the what is known as the eastern United States fell and/or were decimated in the face of the encroachment of "civilization". Confederations such as the Powhatan of the mid Atlantic tidewater region were no more. The Haudenosaunee, the Iroquois Confederacy that once ranged over parts of eastern Canada, New York, and Pennsylvania were greatly reduced from what they once were. Some of their numbers remained on fractions of what was once a vast area of custodianship. Others were to become refugees and forced to migrate westward. Gone were the great mound cities of the southeast and adjacent regions. The length of the period of contact in this area was several centuries old in comparison to the situation that many of the more western peoples were encountering (the southwest being the exception, due to Spanish incursion. This expansion was halted temporarily due to the efforts of the Pueblo man Pope, in 1680. The Spanish push would start again in twelve years in 1692.) Encountering these different cultures required a wide range of diplomatic skills. In some instances, some of these men would find welcome in these societies. Because the nations in general adopted those who were worthy and/or willing to join their ranks, some of these men became members of these nations. There were other situations that arose. White entrepreneurs found it was better to have someone of African descent handle negotiations on their behalf when dealing with the representative(s) of a nation. Thus certain individuals who were familiar with and respectful of cultural protocols, found they were an asset to their employers. In the west, history was repeating itself with a twist. There was a point in time when men and women of African descent living among southeastern nations were valued as translators and interpreters when dealing with entities outside of their respective communities who spoke English, Spanish, or French. As fate had unfolded, in the early years of the establishment of South Carolina, it was enslaved Africans at times, along with a white trader, who navigated the waterways and woods to engage in contact with native Peoples of the region on behalf of their owners. Many of these Africans had become versed in native languages. As there were still some of these African men that had memories of their lives in (primarily) West Africa, the subtropical environment of this region was a familiar one, different, yet similar to the natural conditions on the other side of the Atlantic Ocean. It was this familiarity that was capitalized by those of the ruling class in South Carolina who sought to exploit opportunity wherever it was to be found. This meant agricultural endeavors, such as rice, were to become one of the most profitable of exports, and the trade with the various native peoples, although the latter was to interrupted from time to time because of warfare. When this happened during the early years, the ruling class quickly resorted to slaving with whichever nation it had conflict with supplying the victims. The Tuscarora War of 1711 and the Yamasee War of 1715 are only two examples. More laws passed throughout the south. Time went on that forbid the taking of anyone of African descent into anywhere that there could be contact with native peoples. This was not easy to enforce. Now in regions west of the Mississippi River, men of African descent often filled this role for white employers in dealing with various nations that resided in different areas. With the continued encroachment westward of "civilization" the options and opportunities that once were prevalent to those of color shrank in the face of the onslaught.

Following the War of Independence, the reality of a firm foothold on the territories of the eastern seaboard was a fact. These former English colonies were comprised of thirteen states. Different ventures had put the white inhabitants in touch with various native communities. There had been numerous military clashes for whatever reason, certainly going back over periods that encompassed decades all over the regions. Expansion had been put on hold because of the war. With the cessation of combat, the push west and south was again about to escalate. The concerns of the native communities that were in the path of this expansion for the most part were issues primarily because of the threat of resistance that many communities would implement in their defense. Many of the nations located along the eastern seaboard and the immediate adjacent regions had already experienced this phenomenon. And while word of the fates of these numerous nations had spread into more interior areas through networks that had existed for years, it was now time for these interior communities to bear the brunt of white expansion. Contact with whites was not a new phenomenon. While the 1803 expedition of Lewis and Clark readily comes to mind, they were not unique in that they explored areas unfamiliar to various European entities, vying for a part of what is now North America. English, French, and Spanish men had traveled into these regions over different points in time. Some had come as soldiers, venturing on behalf of their respective nations. Some were individual adventurers, seeking to flee life from wince they came for any number of reasons. One of the main reasons, however, was for profit. Trade was a major factor for contacts. At different points on the wide frontier were trading posts. Traders also traveled into communities. In some instances, these men married native women and would reside among their wives' people. The offspring of these unions and the sociopolitical positions that some of them would rise to were to play a major role in many of the societies from which there mothers came. And while several southeastern nations such as the Creeks, Choctaws, Cherokees and Chickasaws serve as examples, they certainly were not the exclusive cases. In some instances, African men and women lived in some of these communities. The further away from white settlements meant there was a much higher chance of integrating into the community upon which an individual found him or herself. The closer to white settlement always meant a high degree of uncertainty. These native towns were subject to situations that existed in white settlements, and increasingly, these native settlements grew desperate as they tried to cope with effects of racism that were aimed directly at them. Hopes of preventing red-black alliances meant there were constant divide and conquer tactics implemented. There were possibilities of capture and return to white settlements, or death. As in other parts of the country, enslaved Africans would often be used and rewarded in efforts to kill native peoples. For a person of African descent, life among a native community was preferable and certainly far better for the most part than the sociopolitical unstableness of white society had to offer, at least as far as being a person of color was concerned. Some of these men were escaping from enslavement. Some men (in particular) were technically "Free", but realizing the precariousness of this condition in society that condoned and encouraged, in many instances, chattel slavery, they saw that it was better to take their chances elsewhere. Some of these men had first traveled into these areas accompanying white traders. And while it was law in many states that it was forbidden to take enslaved men into native communities, it was a law that was difficult to enforce. During the colonial period in some areas it was African men that initially had traveled on their owners behalves to different native communities. This diminished as fears of red-black alliances began to grow in the minds of the ruling class. Those settlements that were located on coastal regions of what was to become the United States had their anxieties fed on a regular basis. Reports for different parts of the Caribbean consistently tell of not only revolt attempts by enslaved peoples, but also of towns established by those victims of enslavement who had managed for whatever period of time to attempt to create situations more favorable to their own beings, as precarious as that may have been. Reports from the Virgin Islands and Saint Kitts in 1734 of revolts, were not necessarily unique in that victims of the slave system continually rebelled when possible, throughout the hemisphere. The treaty negotiated with maroons in Jamaica in 1738 probably was responsible for numerous nightmares among the slaveholding classes throughout the areas where colonization had taken place. So to create and maintain tensions between red and black offered varying degrees of security.

When the southeast is examined, we begin to see seeds of discontent, as over time those descendants who were born of white fathers and native mothers would gain political influence, and the ideals that were espoused by this growing faction would start to bring social upheaval. Thus, the phenomenon of the "Progressives versus the Traditionalists" began. Some of the characteristics of this situation can be observed by looking at the governing mechanisms that had been in place in any given area. Generally speaking, it was the council system that held sway over many matters. There were variations, depending on which nation (Creek, Cherokee etc.) observed, but most had this in common. Decisions were reached by consensus, and the council would try to avoid any action that might bring disharmony to the community. Similarly, the "Chief" was the voice of the people, and for the most part could not take any course of action by coercion. This man would sit at the head of the council, but the traditions called for choices that would benefit the community without disrupting the peace. And while the council was comprised of men, (in the east) the councils existed in the context of matrilineal society. In some cases, it was through an elder respected woman's family that a chief was chosen; similarities are found in the northeast as well as the southeast among Muskogean, Iroquoian, and Algonquin peoples. As important as the council system, if not more so, was the Clan. The Clan was the central part of life for many southeastern people. Each Clan camp was under the watchful eye of a matriarch. In this camp would reside wives and husbands, sons in law, children, aged relatives, and sometimes orphans and war captives. The importance of the role of women in southeastern societies was not always restricted to the settlements. Among the Cherokee, the War Woman would accompany the warriors on the warpath. While there were some domestic duties to which she was obligated, she was the first person responsible for the decision of executing or keeping alive prisoners of war, and her advise was valued in councils. Between the clan and the council system, the needs and concerns of the community were taken care of. As white traders began to enter these communities the dynamics would start to alter. As fate would have it, some of these traders entering into various indigenous settlements were of Scottish or Irish ancestry, in which a cultural trait was that of belonging to a specific clan.

Here was the common thread. One didn't have to look far by the turn of the nineteenth century to find Scottish and Irish surnames in southeastern communities. But there was also distinct differences. Many sons that had white fathers would adopt the European custom of inheriting property from the father. This was the exact opposite of what had been the tradition in most southeastern indigenous communities. There was also the tendency by some of these individuals to look out for their own interests. This was not always the case. There were men of this biracial heritage that were loyal to their mother's people. Yet it was some of those individuals with this lineage who would often side with the interests of white colonists, especially where there was something in it for themselves. As these men had gained prestige because of the legacy left to them and as many of them continued to build their respective businesses, some began to have increasing influence in their community's council. As more of these individuals gained positions on the council(s), a distinct point of view became prevalent. It was among these individuals that further acculturation toward Eurocentric values was taking place, at times complete with the frame of mind that often mimicked their white neighbors. It was here that these people were observed owning chattel slaves, and in most instances their homes could not be distinguished from the southern white aristocracy. It would also be this faction of the respective councils that the United States Government would approach presuming for whatever reason that these factions spoke for the entire community when, in reality, nothing could have been further from the truth. This elite faction were the ones that would jump at opportunities not necessarily beneficial to the entire community. Yet when examining how respective communities were being affected, it is seen that there were factions that wished to adhere to values that had been lived by for generations, and these factions came into direct conflict with the mindset that had found its way into the community. Indeed, we see some indigenous people who found advantages in victimizing Africans; increasingly, in the eighteenth and nineteenth centuries this group of people would be almost exclusively the elite faction. Some warriors would take Africans to be sold or traded elsewhere among white settlements. However, not all of the people who were enslaved or taken to slavers to be sold into bondage by elements within Cherokee society were of African ancestry. As this elite cadre had gained some degree of sociopolitical control in the culture, those that were deemed opposition or problematic for whatever reason could find themselves enroute to the auction blocks of Charleston or elsewhere as the enforcers for the will of the elite terrorized communities throughout the settlements of Cherokee country. As it would happen among some of the southeastern nations these circumstances, along with other factors would continue to stir social discontent and turmoil among the population to the point where civil unrest occurred time and time again, not only in the southeast but (after the forced relocation of the southeastern peoples) in Indian Territory/Oklahoma as bloodshed would take place among opposing factions. In the instance of the Cherokees, this was to occur until 1846, although the same dynamics that had split into three distinct factions were to fuel more animosity during the American Civil War. Among the Creeks, factionalism had precipitated the Civil War of 1813-14, and would provide the roots of hostilities during the American Civil War, and eventually lead to the Green Peach War of 1882-3 and the Crazy Snake Uprisings of 1901 and 1907. There would be retentions of some attitudes that are identified with the old south by factions of the "Five Civilized Tribes". Such was the case of factionalism in the Southeast and in Oklahoma.

As time went on there were reports of negative treatments of Africans. Yet if we look closely at what happened initially and well throughout the 1800s most Cherokees were humane toward those brought into their midst. Early colonist in North and South Carolina reported that their slaves were being stolen by Cherokees. There were also reports that people of African descent were living comfortably (relative to the time period) among Cherokee communities, especially when those communities were more geographically isolated from European settlements. It was among these communities where the inhabitants had not strayed far from their traditional values that other people (outsiders) would be taken into the community. Regardless of how whatever faction looked upon those of African descent in their midst, some of these new members of the community proved to have valuable skills. One of these skills was multilingualism. Many of these new community members not only spoke the language of the people, but languages of the European settlers: English, French, and Spanish.

In some cases, the "interpreter" spoke more than one indigenous language, as some communities were part of a larger confederacy which, in some cases, were multilingual such as the Creeks and, to a certain extent, the people who were to be eventually known as Seminoles. This same dynamic would continue to be a factor in Oklahoma after the forced relocations of the 1830s,40s. Here the survivors of the Trail of Tears were of all types of complexions and hair textures. Although as time would passed there would be other people moving into "Indian Territory", already in place were populations that were culturally Cherokee, Creek, Chickasaw, or Seminole, that were multiracial. In some instances there were specific towns that were black or comprised of those that were of African/Native ancestry. This was most prevalent among the Seminoles and Creeks. In Florida, we find that there were often black settlements adjacent to indigenous settlements. These communities were autonomous with their own ruling structures, and in turn, they were within the jurisdiction of the larger indigenous community. Alachua, Tallahasse, Suwanee, and Lake Miccosukee are some examples of this. There were also reports from white travelers in Florida that there were some black settlements that were beholden only to themselves. Florida was not unique in this way, although it may be the most documented. Reports from other locales that had areas that were by definition inaccessible stated that there were settlements of runaway slaves. This was reported from parts of North and South Carolina, Mississippi, Alabama, Georgia, and Virginia. One such community in Virginia found itself surrounded by events beyond its control. During the late Spring - early Summer of 1862, soldiers of the United States and the Confederate States were locked in combat in an area outside of Richmond Virginia called "Indian Country". George Alfred Townsend, a reporter for the New York Herald, reported in 1862 that on an island in the Pamunkey River its residents were "half breeds" and mixed Indians and negroes from Indiantown. These were people of Pamunkey-Mattaponi ancestry who were within visual range of units of both armies of the Confederate States of America, as well as the United States of America. Where this community was located was of vital strategic importance to the conflicting forces.

The slave trade was a horrible phenomenon. Africans as well as indigenous peoples were the victims of this institution, which lasted for centuries. The number of native victims enslaved would decrease as more Africans were routed into the system, but did not disappear entirely. The fear of an alliance of red and black was real to the minds of the slaveholding class. If indigenous people were, in any significant numbers enslaved alongside of African victims, the grounds for such alliances were born. Indeed, there were, throughout the era of early colonization of the hemisphere by Europeans, indigenous communities that adopted Africans into their respective societies.

Maroon settlements were also prevalent. This would occur wherever there was sufficient isolation, and the members of those communities could live far from oppression, although constantly alert. These settlements were often comprised of African and native people. It became practical in the eastern seaboard to downplay the enslavement of indigenous people, and/or ship out any native person to points in the Caribbean to be enslaved if, for no other reason, a military alliance between red and black could have dire consequences for those in power. This was proven during the Seminole Wars, as well as other confrontations that have gone unnoticed by mainstream history while the communities fighting against oppression fell to military pressure. It was determined after a time that (in the United States), it was more practical to deal in an enslaved labor pool of Africans as opposed to indigenous people. Another result of the slave trade was that on islands off of West Africa, such as Cape Verde, people that were to suffer the horrors enslavement would come together by no choice. Among these numbers were Native American people that had fallen victim to this tragic circumstance. Thus, in scenarios similar to what was happening on islands in the Caribbean, men, women, and children from different parts of the world such as the Americas, Africa and to an extent Asia, interacted under the yoke of enslavement. As the institution that characterized chattel slavery diminished through the course of the nineteenth century in the western hemisphere, the largescale movement of the colonization of Africa (as well as Asia) shifted into high gear. In the United States, efforts continued to undermine native sovereignty in Indian Territory, eventually usurping and collapsing the social structures that had evolved in this region. This was to lead to the establishment of the state of Oklahoma.

Where the outright enslavement of people has ceased (in most areas of the world) during modern times, other forms of oppression has substituted. Indigenous communities in Central and South America located in rurally remote areas of their respective countries have been attacked by agents of military dictatorships and, in some instances also attacked by entities fighting those dictatorships. There are parallels that are drawn to the communities of African Americans who witnessed nightridings (a unique form of domestic terrorism) well into the 20th century in some communities, to the mass attacks characterized in situations like (but not limited to) Tulsa, Oklahoma, in 1921 and Rosewood, Florida, in 1923 (communities in Florida were subject to attacks during the early and mid 1800s; eventually, the intense escalation of hostilities would become known as the Seminole Wars). While the events that took place in Tulsa certainly has gained their place in infamy, other towns in Oklahoma had already suffered similar fates by this point in time. It turns out that many of these towns similar to Tulsa were originally settlements located within the Creek and Cherokee Nations. Here government officials were well aware of what was happening but made slow, token efforts to intervene while events were rapidly unfolding. Indigenous communities in the United States were certainly no strangers to having their communities attacked from outsiders. It still is not unusual for indigenous communities to be threatened by violence from outsiders. Chiapas, Mexico is but one example as this reality is a fact throughout the hemisphere in the late twentieth century. The Zapatistas struggle paid off to some extent, as members of this group marched into Mexico City and met with the federal government in March of 2001 to demand justice and peace with dignity for their people. Even into the 21rst century, one hears of people of color being exploited, working for long hours for poor pay at urban and rural sweatshops around the world, while reports of slavery tragically continue to come out of regions of South America and East Africa.

Points West: Indian Territory and Beyond.

The Indian Removal Act of 1830 would further traumatize many nations of the east. The pattern was already established. Indeed throughout the hemisphere native communities continued to be eradicated. There were survivors that remained in the east. Some Choctaw, Creek, Cherokee, Seminole, (and other peoples) found sanctuary in areas that were at best classified as inaccessible. In some instances, individuals would blend into white or black societies. Although small groups managed to survive in areas that were marginalized and/or had proved to be undesirable in the eyes of the expanding dominant culture, no individual or groups were truly safe. In what is known as North Carolina, South Carolina, Alabama, Georgia, Mississippi, and Florida, it was clear to the intent of white expansion that the indigenous communities within these areas would have to be eliminated. By this point in time this attitude was firmly established as a rule and was to continue to move westward. In the case of the people of the various eastern communities, Indian Territory was to be the place where those who survived were to end up. The tribulations that were to be encountered by these refugees were often beyond horrific. The displacements certainly were traumatic enough, yet the sorrow of this occurrence was to increase. Many people were to die horrible deaths on what was to be called the Trail of Tears. As had been the case many times before and tragically would not cease until the Pacific Coast was reached, the native communities that stood in the way of the routes of expansion had to go. The way that this was to be accomplished really didn't matter. Senecas, Lenapes, Oneidas, Mandan, Sac, Fox, Wyandot, Potawatomis,and Pawnees, along with other nations, were to face the horrors that came with forced removal. Thousands of native lives were to be lost. Part of the residual effects of this was that native nations would come into conflicts. In some of the nations of the southeast, there had already existed for decades sociopolitical situations that widened the gap between factions within the respective communities. Among the Cherokee, Creek, and Choctaw, violence would erupt in scenarios that are best described as a civil war. And some of these strong, divergent points of view were to again rise up into violence during the years of national regeneration once the peoples had been relocated. Civil strife among the Cherokees and Creeks are sadly the examples to examine: the last outbreak of civil hostilities would be among the Creeks in 1907 which, in of itself was a pivotal period for the nations living in the boundaries of this region. When these southeastern peoples were first relocated in the area(s), they were to come into conflict with several other nations that historically lived and traversed the region. These specific nations were at odds with each other from time to time, and the fact that there were now newcomers in the mix only meant (in the eyes of some) that there was increased competition for the resources the land had to offer. Early contacts with bands of Pawnee, Lakotas, Osage, and Comanches were not pleasant events. As time passed, the governments of the southeastern nations were to send diplomatic emissaries to these different groups of Plains people on a continual basis in the hopes of reaching an understanding. A convention was held at Talequah in what was now the Cherokee Nation (in Indian Territory) during 1843. Thousands gathered from many different nations to encourage good relations throughout the region. Representatives from some Plains bands were present. Eventually, this area designated Indian Territory was to be known as Oklahoma.

The War of Independence that was fought between England and its colonies in the Americas certainly made its impact felt on the native cultures of North America. One point of impact was economical. Traditional trade routes were disrupted as a result of hostilities. This caused a domino effect, as it became difficult in this atmosphere to conduct business. The fact that business was not as usual was felt throughout the continent. The nations in the immediate vicinities of hostility were the most heavily effected. Native alliances with either the British or the upstart colonists wreaked havoc and caused communities to split. The roots of some of the Cherokee civil upheavals of the 1800s were established in this period. Disillusioned with what was felt as bad decisions by elders such as Oconostota, Savanukah, and Attakullakulla, a faction of younger Cherokee championed by Dragging Canoe (who was the son of Attakullakulla) would lead and establish several towns along Chickamauga Creek, Tennessee. The older leaders had seen and experienced bloodshed throughout their lives. These men had seen battle on numerous occasions over the years. Yet with the onslaught triggered by people who would be known as Americans, these elders felt there had been enough blood spilled, and sought to preserve what was best for the Cherokee as a whole. This sentiment was not shared by all. The communities that followed Dragging Canoe pledged never to seek compliance with the Americans. Dragging Canoe's followers would become known as the Chickamauga. This faction was characterized by their steadfast cultural conservatism and spirit of resistance. They, along with the Kituwahs, were to champion and maintain as much as possible the traditional ways of the people. With the relocation of the people to the west, it was inevitable that there would be conflicts among the population. Yet the roots of the conflicts had been established in the southeastern homelands. Alliances were not a new phenomenon. Native warriors had fought with and against (at varying times and locations) the French, English, Spanish, Dutch, etc. But the impact of war was felt throughout the continent. The trade network had been hemispheric in scope at the time of the invasion of the west.

With the onslaught of European entities spilling blood, this scope had narrowed. With the commencement of this particular conflict, the flow of goods and numerous resources that had been usually distributed by trade became the victim of a domino effect that started in the east and was felt in all other directions north, south, and west. The normal flow of goods was again interrupted, and, in step with events of the times, would never recover to the degree of its former degree. When the civil war is examined, the result is no less devastating in its cost to the lives of those who were the residents of many indigenous nations.

The Cherokees, historically, were comprised of more than sixty towns that encompassed parts of present day Tennessee, Kentucky, Virginia, North Carolina, South Carolina, Alabama, and Georgia. The Creeks had more than 54 towns spread out over Alabama and Georgia. The Choctaws were largely in Mississippi, and also spread into parts of Louisiana, Alabama, Georgia and Florida (the Choctaws were the first of the southeastern people to be forced from their homelands in 1831-32). The Chickasaws encompassed areas of Mississippi, Tennessee, Kentucky, and Arkansas. The peoples who were to become known as Seminoles, were occupying areas of North and Central Florida. Larger numbers of whites were moving into areas throughout the region(s) east of the Mississippi River. The thrust from the coastlines meant there was only one way to go, and this movement was clearly aimed at more interior regions. Ironically it would not solely be the lust for land that proved to be the downfall for so many. Among the southeastern nations were an elite that had mimicked white society. It was the elites' sociopolitical success, and the influences that the spawned in their respective societies that made Americans feel uneasy. The Creek, Choctaw, and Cherokee nations had established schools and had business enterprises that were modeled (to whatever degree) after white counterparts. These institutions and lifestyles had equaled, and in some instances surpassed their white counterparts (in the minds of some), and regardless of the fact that these institutions were successful within their respective societies, some white Americans felt threatened. Yet among those societies were elements that didn't agree with the way things had materialized among this elite group. By and large the majority of the populations within these nations were more inclined to be culturally conservative and distance themselves from the elite. Long before the dreaded Trail of Tears, some Cherokees decided to take their chances out west and left to settle in what was being called Indian Territory.

Others traveled to other points, notably south toward Mexico where some believed that the ancestors had originally migrated from in times past. This first group that remained in Indian Territory would eventually be known as the Old Settlers, and there was to be strong, factional disputes for years when others joined them (these being survivors of the Trail of Tears). Some of this factionalism existed in the southeast, and there were times when violence would erupt behind issues. Choctaws, Chickasaws, Creeks, and Cherokees would see these civil conflicts explode into bloodshed. The lines were drawn (in many of the nations) into these two groups: The Traditionals, and the "Progressives" (Assimilationists). This prompted some to seek alternatives by relocating elsewhere. This meant that the best alternative was to migrate westward.

The Old Settler Cherokees were culturally conservative. Some of these Cherokees began migrating during the late 1700s, heading for areas of Louisiana,

Texas, Arkansas, Missouri, and what is now Oklahoma. There were periods of violence between this group and bands of Osage. Initially, the areas where some members of this group of Cherokees settled was in contested territory that various bands of Osage had (in their eyes) custodianship. Indeed, many areas of Indian Country were contested by some of the aforementioned nomadic and semi nomadic bands of Plains people. So the Old Settler Cherokees, like other transplanted southeastern peoples who came after them, initially found out the hard way that they were new players in the area, whether they liked it or not, and there were instances of early contacts between peoples who were anything but pleasant. Even after a treaty was signed by representatives of both peoples in St.Louis during 1819, the bloodshed continued. Geographically, the southeastern nations resettling the area had their own sections of land where their respective nations were located. The Chickasaws and the Choctaws were the most southern of the nations, with the Chickasaws being west and the Choctaws east.

Up to the period of the civil war, transplanted Chickasaw settlements were the target of frequent horse raids. Different bands of Comanche traveled out of Texas and other southwestern points to wreak havoc on these settlements, which were in many instances just north of the Texas line. It seems that the (relocated) Chickasaw was the nation just north of the Texas border. It was not unusual to have possees of Chickasaw, Choctaw, etc., to launch pursuits in attempts to regain their property. The Texas-Indian Territory border was to be a crossroad for a long time to come, with traffic going northward as well as southward for any number of reasons. As fate would have it, a cattle route that was to run from Texas northward to the upper portion of Indian Territory into Kansas where the railroad yards were located would become known by the name of the Cherokee man who paved the way: The Chisolm Trail.

Once in Indian Territory, the nations (as they would come to be known) faced the task of rebuilding their lives. Most had difficulties growing directly from the result of these removal forced upon them by the United States Government. Many had lost members of community during the course of removals, and in some instances these losses were measured in the thousands. Compounding this was the fact that goods and supplies necessary for survival were often late in arriving and, at times, once they did arrive, they proved to be of inferior quality and in short supply. Internal political strife was sometimes fanned by actions taken by federal officials, civilian and military. Some government officials went as far as to start rumors of pending actions by warriors of different nations so that there could be the possibility of direct military intervention on the part of the U.S. Army. General Matthew Arbuckle seemed to have this pattern of behavior down to a science. This happened on several occasions to the Cherokees.

Representatives of varying factions within respective nations (Seminole, Cherokee, etc.) spent a great deal of time transiting the long route between Indian Territory and Washington, D.C., to jockey for whatever resources that could be obtained from the federal government. These representatives also continued to make the case (or cases, in some instances) why their particular faction was the one that truly had their respective peoples' interest at heart. The period of the

1840s and 50s saw this movement of statesmen from Indian Territory. Outlawed elements coming from nearby white settlements saw that the vast region of Indian Territory often was a place to hole up between misadventures and mayhem, as various indigenous police units (known as Lighthorse), the U.S. Army, and after the civil war, the U.S. Marshals, had their hands more than full, attempting to maintain control over this vast area. As time passed, these lawmen of various shades of skin color and hair textures found that they were often in pursuit of outlaws of various skin colors and hair textures. Some of the new arrivals in the territory had to deal with the new environment at times of ecological turmoil such as drought, severe winters, and the resulting aftermaths of such phenomenon. Yet the human spirit is one of rising to meet the face of adversity. In spite of what was thrown at them by nature and man, the people persevered, at a cost, but yet, persevered. As structures and institutions rebounded in the attempt to deal with the real concern of living, old rivalries and conflicts let it be known that there were issues that, if not resolved, would remain difficult to solve. Governing mechanisms that arose in this region blended degrees of traditional structures with concepts of Eurocentric-style government (in the model of the United States). To a large degree, this process had already started back in the southeastern homelands. The faction(s) that had adopted Eurocentric-style governing mechanisms had an element that was certainly at odds with those that were considered more culturally conservative. In Indian Territory, this faction again became the entity that the United States Government and later the Confederate States of America turned to deal with issues affecting the communities now residing in this area. Residually, there were still, among the varying nations conservative factions that would continue to distance themselves as much as possible from the assimilationist faction. To a degree, the conservatives (Traditionalists) were able to accomplish this, but time and time again, situations and issues would come to the forefront that had to be addressed. At times, longstanding grudges had simmered just beneath the surface of the respective societies, only to erupt into violence at different points in time. This was especially true for the Cherokee and Creek. One of the ongoing issues was that of those of African descent living in the societies. Both freeborn and enslaved found themselves caught up in social turmoil that would continue to escalate. Ruling bodies in the territory became increasingly oppressive. Laws were enacted that were to prove detrimental to anyone of African descent. Intermarriage was outlawed among some of the nations as early as the 1840s. This proved to be difficult to enforce, as many people in their respective cultures who fell in the mindset of being "Traditionalist" tended to conduct themselves by the ways of their ancestors and ignore the rulings set forth by governing bodies that increasingly mimicked the ways of the southern white aristocracy. There was a domino effect as far as these laws were concerned. The hardening of laws in one nation would often lead to similar situations in neighboring nations. Among the Cherokees and Choctaws, their respective governing bodies passed legislation making life more difficult for those of African descent. Because of this, there was an exodus during the 1850s into the Creek Nation of those seeking to leave adversity behind. By the latter part of the 1850s the Creek Nation began to pass similar legislation as its neighbors. No doubt that these actions were to stem the flow of refugees into the Creek Nation, as well as stiffen sociopolitical conditions of those of African descent who had been longtime residence of the nation, free or enslaved. Although there existed a faction that was escalating its attitudes toward those of African descent in negative ways, Seminoles still had a tendency to stick together. Upon their arrival in Indian Territory many Seminoles (largely but not exclusively Creek-Seminoles) at first lived in what was Cherokee Nation. In its brilliant wisdom the United States government attempted to bring relocated Seminoles under the control of the Creek Nation. This was to be partially accomplished (in theory) by placing Seminoles in the Creek Nation. There was still strong animosities in place, and this match was bound for trouble from the start. One Creek law forbade anyone of African descent from bearing arms. Other nations would enact similar laws. During the earlier years of relocation, many people in general kept firearms close by as there was the ongoing threat of attack by any number of warriors from some of the Plains people that transited the area(s). Those of African descent among some communities were granted access to guns but, in some instances the weapons were not immediately available on an ongoing basis. It was widely known that Seminoles owned guns. This certainly applied to all male Seminoles, regardless of complexion. The presence of (armed) black Seminoles in particular that lived among the nation created a situation that the Creek Council wanted to control but didn't want to risk the wrath of these settlements whose warriors had proven themselves to be formidable. Even with the rise of factionalism among Seminoles, it became clear (on principal) that these communities would stand together against any outside threat. This reality was the case during the early days of resettlement. Eventually, there were factions among the Seminoles that took the same position as the Creek Council, although they, too, were not willing to move against the black towns. Some elements among the Creek Council tried to get the aid of the United States Army to intervene. At the time that this was happening, Marcellus Duvall, a man who played a role in pursuing Billy Bowlegs and his band in Florida during 1849, was approached by the Creek Council and some opposing Seminoles to handle the situation of dealing with black Seminole communities in particular. The U.S. Army was reluctant to press the issue by use of force, for it was known that the promise to defend its communities was one that the majority of Seminoles would not hesitate to do. Not willing to start a full- scale war in the territory, General Matthew Arbuckle refused to issue orders that would have Army personnel attempt to disarm the black Seminole towns. Living conditions there had begun to resemble those that had taken place in Florida, as black Seminoles established their own towns. Upon the establishment of these semi autonomous towns, the residents began a constant vigilance for slavers (of varying complexions). Those who were watching these towns felt uneasy, not only because of these communities were armed, but it was feared that these areas would become a beacon for runaway slaves from the surrounding areas, regardless of complexion. Some community leaders of prominence such as John Horse, were the victim of assassination and enslavement attempts. John Horses' longtime ally, WildCat was in similar danger because of his actions in the territory and elsewhere. The relationship between the two men reached back into Florida. Together, they had seen trail and tribulation, including the escape from the fortress prison of Fort Marion in Saint Augustine. This was at the time when the patriot Osceola was being held prisoner prior to being shipped out to South Carolina, where he was to die from illness.

The interaction of the numerous Plains and prairie peoples with the relocated southeastern peoples was complex. There was already a schism between Traditionalists and Assimilationist factions among the nations of the southeast. The differences had led and would continue to lead to upheavals that, in some cases lasted into the beginning of the twentieth century. Contact with the western peoples would further be as complex if not more so for similar reasons. The elite of the major southeastern nations had taken on characteristics of the southern white aristocracy, while trying to hold on to the native identity(ies). The culturally conservative Traditionals mindset was at direct odds with this type of conscienceness. The western peoples that began to come in contact with the southeastern peoples now in areas they felt were under their custodianship because of historic trading and hunting efforts, felt autonomous over time. They answered (for the time being) only to their own cultural protocols. Observing some of the southeastern peoples in their homes and their ways, felt like they were observing people who had sold out to the encroaching white society. The "elite" of the southeastern nations, already feeling socially superior to their own kinspeople who continued to hold on to the old ways, felt they now were truly in jeopardy from "wild Indians". It is said that Peter Pitchlynn, a leader of the Choctaws, held views of some of the western peoples which bordered on contempt. There are conflicting stories of how early negotiations in November of 1838 between Osage Leader Pawhuska and Peter Pitchlynn's delegation went. Initial accounts close after the event reported there were fruitful interchanges. Later accounts, as reported in the Cherokee Phoenix in 1877, had Peter Pitclynn speaking to the Osage in threatening terms. While these reports bear scrutiny, it can be assumed that there existed a mindset on behalf of some southeastern people that looked down on the Plains people and vice versa. Interestingly enough, early peaceful interactions with the western peoples were more successful when southeastern Traditionalists were involved in exchanges. There was some common ground, as both parties were honestly engaged in the attempt to hold on (in a conservative sense) to their customs. And while there would be continued tensions from time to time for a variety of reasons, at least from the standpoint of mutual respect for cultural integrity, there could be some meaningful exchange that was mutually beneficial. One example was that of the exchanges that existed between WildCat of the Seminoles and bands of the Comanche and Kickapoos.

WildCat and his band had been through their share of tribulations while in Florida. He himself had proven time and time again to be a cunning warrior. While still in Florida, WildCat and his some members of his band were captured after a parley and transplanted to Indian Territory by November of 1841. It was not until March of 1843 when he and his followers were settled on lands that had been assigned to them. This brought WildCat into close proximity with various bands of Plains people. WildCat's diplomacy was to prove beneficial, as in 1849 he and John Horse would lead an exodus out of Indian Territory south into Mexico with little interference during the early part of the journey from Plains people who spanned areas through where the travelers would pass. As discontent grew because of the climate of attitudes in Indian Territory, WildCat began to journey south toward Mexico, establishing contacts with indigenous peoples along the way, such as different Comanche and Kickapoo bands. WildCat had actually come to have some familiarity with the region as he had traveled in the area on hunting and diplomatic missions in the past. During his diplomatic endeavors, he had earned the trust of the peoples he had contacted, as he was still closely in touch with his traditions. This fact was a strong influence in his relating to the southern Plains people, as they had come to distrust those that they felt were living like "white men" (assimilationists). Those of the Plains cultures felt a common bond with WildCat, and his honest and frank dealing had paid off in the gaining of a positive status. This was crucial as he and John Horse led an exodus out of Indian Territory, bound for Mexico. In July of 1849, the Mexican Government let it be known that for those willing to establish colonies on the eastern and western frontiers of the country, supplies would be issued to assist in the establishment of towns. These supplies included oxen, horses, six months of provisions, and tools. Given what was felt like the growing instability of events in Indian Territory, this offer was a tempting incentive. The first of these exoduses commenced on November 10, 1849. This first group was not to reach Mexico until July of 1850, settling on lands granted by the Mexican Government in Coahuila. This group of refugees would encounter hostility as they neared the Texas-Mexico border from Comanche warriors who were not affiliated with the bands who WildCat had established relations with. Not only did Seminoles travel with John Horse and WildCat, but so did Cherokees and Creeks of varying complexions and hair textures who felt increasing discomfort because of policies being set forth by those who were in political control. There were also Kickapoos who joined the travelers. It seemed better to take chances, heading across woods and prairie to the possibility of building a better life, than to stay in an environment increasingly (in some areas) starting to resemble the old south. Subsequent journeys by other hopeful refugees would be even less fortunate. Other exoduses faced more frequent hazards, as various groups harried the travelers. A group of refugees led by Jim Bowlegs had to contend with a band of Comanches that who were to capture and kill some of his party. On his final trip out of Indian Territory, WildCat would be pursued by Creek LightHorsemen, as well as other men looking to capitalize on whatever could be taken by force. Texas Rangers as well as other representatives of law enforcement knew there was a profit to be made by capturing and selling anyone of African descent who was trying to get to Mexico (Ironically a black Seminole was to join the Texas Rangers, the law enforcement agency, in the 1990's). The communities in Mexico would come to comprise with Seminoles, Creeks, Cherokees, Kickapoos, Biloxis, and other peoples of color who decided to take their chances on this frontier.

And while there were social upheavals happening with the Seminoles because of where and who they had been relocated among, the Creeks had established for the most part good relations with the various Plains people with whom they were in contact. In later years, there were to be intermarriages between these diverse groups of people. The Seminoles and the Creeks were geographically located on the westernmost fringes of Indian Territory. Cherokees, Choctaws, and Chickasaws were more located in the eastern regions of the territory, thus, numerically speaking, they had less immediate contact with the Plains people. Since there were people who had African ancestry among the southeastern nations spanning the social spectrum, the exchanges with the western peoples would also play a role in their existence. At times, this meant violent interaction as in the case of raids on settlements. In the earliest years of relocation there was a wide variety of problems confronting the uprooted people.

The threat of bloodshed from outside warriors was one of the most immediate. The fear of raids was a reality. There was a need to defend oneself and community. Yet some of the raids were not necessarily a question of seeking blood, per se. Horse stealing was an honorable undertaking for many western peoples, and the lure of horse herds would time and time again prove irresistible for young men in particular looking to gain prominent status among their respective communities. And long after there was a ceasing of blood raids, the quest to obtain horses and the amount of mischief caused by the theft of this kind of property was to prove a colossal headache over and over again. After the civil war, Indian Territory would encounter additional problems brought on by the fact of being a vast territory with open borders. This proved to be ideal for outlaws of all types of complexions. A tactic of white horse thieves was to make their actions look like those of any number of western people who had engaged in the action of theft.

It was not new however to have attempts of leaving Indian Territory take place by those who felt there was nothing to lose and more to gain. In the spring of 1842, slaves of Joseph Vann in the Cherokee Nation locked up members of the family and attempted to reach Mexico. The refugees were captured after they had been pursued for three days and fought a two-day battle. The leaders of this attempt were executed. In the aftermath of this attempt to leave the territory, the Cherokee Council passed an act, ordering all free Africans who had not been freed by a Cherokee Nation resident to vacate the nation by January 1, 1843. As fate had it, there were to be at times violent confrontations between some wealthy Cherokee cattlemen and black Creek members of the Creek LightHorse after the Civil War. With the establishment of the Seminole Nation in 1856 and the granting of their own autonomy, this issue diffused somewhat. For those who remained in Indian Territory, they were to find themselves swept up in events that would lead to the horrors of the American Civil War. Regarding the black Seminoles in the territory, with their two strongest advocates now gone (WildCat and John Horse) things were bound to get worse. All residents would fall victim to sociopolitical circumstances, whether they liked it or not. No one of African descent could rest easy. Members of the Beam family who had been living as free people among the Choctaw, Creek, and Seminole, fell victim to slave raiders, and over the next two decades would be the center of controversy. Originally living among the Choctaw, the Beams relocated to Indian Territory during the Choctaw Removal of 1833. The family broke off into smaller units and spread out to better shield themselves from slave raids. This course of action happened after a raid in 1840 left one family member dead and four others kidnapped and sold into slavery in Texas. Initially, the first few of the free Beams were the descendants of a Choctaw named William Beams and his slave, Nellie. All of the children from these parents were given freedom. John Davis of Mississippi laid claim to the Beams and went to great lengths to obtain them, at first, sending agents after them in Indian Territory in 1836, 1839, and 1840. In 1854, Davis wanted the Fugitive Slave Law to be used against the Beams. By invoking this law and obtaining federal backing, it would be possible to begin extradition proceedings against the Beam family. Another example of the deteriorating situation in Indian Territory was seen on February 29, 1861. The Creek Council passed a law stating that free people of African descent had ten days to select a (Creek) master. It was not permissible to choose a white person for this role. Those not complying with this ruling were to be sold for a period of twelve months term to the highest bidder. There was a marked increase in slave hunters into the nations. This included whites who were eyeing people of African descent residing in the nations. But even though there was an increase in these types of ventures, it became acknowledged among slave hunters that "Indian Negroes" made poor slaves by white standards. As conditions deteriorated in Indian Territory, the social situations didn't rival the condition of the enslaved population that was among white society. In the eyes of whites, "Indians" were kinder to their slaves. Whites traveling through the different nations were shocked many times to observe master and slave, working side by side. This was a rarity in white society. Because of perceived leniency and (comparative) lack of restriction that was in existence in Indian Territory, this appeared to be in opposition to the kind of bondage readily identified and institutionalized by the southern white elite. Those of African descent who had lived among Native Americans were labeled as more difficult to control.

Things were escalating. The results were to be equally tragic, regardless of what faction one belonged to, sympathized with, or if one was apathetic to the events encompassing his or her respective community. The tidal wave of war was building. Because of the vast size of the territory, those residing in more isolated locations tended to do as they pleased, and this fact continually frustrated those who had gained a political upper hand time and time again. The issue of slavery was one that continued to divide some of these relocated communities. Just as the elite faction saw and used this institution to their advantage, others opposed slavery and refused to adhere to laws passed by their respective government which in their opinion didn't represent them in the first place. Into this situation was the activities of various Abolitionist factions that were active in different communities of the territory. The elite class in particular saw the actions of these groups, who were often Christian missionaries as a direct threat to their interests. Like their white slaveholding counterparts, the elite believed the deeds of the missionaries was totally detrimental. Some of the missionaries favored integrated church services. Other missionaries had also been teaching some slaves to read.

The distinction must be made clear that many Traditionalists did not except Christianity. While many Traditionalists didn't particularly care for the message of Christianity, the Abolitionists found a receptive audience among these culturally conservative factions as far as opposition to slavery was concerned. The roots of these feelings went back to the days of settlement in the southeast. Some of the opposition to Christianity was theological, as some clung fast to traditional, spiritual practices. Some leaders in their respective communities felt the missionaries' preaching might undermine their sphere of influence. Indeed, some Traditionalists, being true to their sense of cultural conservatism, at times took actions against the missionaries. Yet many Traditionalists felt that chattel slavery had no place in their lives. There continued to be intermarriage between those of African descent and indigenous people. The laws forbidding these unions were easier to legislate than enforce. As fate would have it, the state of Oklahoma in 1907 would enact legislation forbidding intermarriage as one of its first actions. As there was still an atmosphere where land was being allotted to those who met the definition of "Indian" by government standards, these kinds of actions attempted to further legislate whole communities out of existence. Where it was to the benefit of federal representatives to manipulate population statistics, it was done to the detriment on indigenous communities. This was a continuation of the Dawes Commission which, in the late 1880s parceled out land (one hundred sixty acres) to individuals, thus setting the stage for the eventual abolishment of tribal governments such as the Creek, Seminole Cherokee, Choctaw, Chickasaw etc., and the communities as an entity. When the federal authorities finally decided the tribal governments had to go,(setting things in motion from a "legal" standpoint), these governing bodies had little recourse, if any. So much for the guise of respecting sovereignty.

As events in the United States continued to escalate, elements of the United States Government and the entity that was to be known as the Confederate States of America eyed the Indian Territory as a source of manpower that could be used on the battlefield. The slaveholding class of the "Five Civilized Tribes" had lifestyles that had some elements of the cultures from which they had descended, as well as traits that were readily identifiable with the old south. These factions were the ones that pledged allegiance to the envoys representing the Confederate States of America. Elements within these factions had already come to positions of prominence in their respective societies. Yet within the respective cultures of the Cherokee, Choctaw, Creek, Chickasaw, and Seminole were those who felt their interests were better served with the United States. A more common point of view was of wanting to be left alone from the entire affair. No one was to be that fortunate, and the tide of war swept up all residents of Indian Territory. In some instances, the split that happened among each respective culture occurred where there had been factionalism that traced its roots back into the southeast.

The Cherokees had witnessed sectarian violence that continued until 1848. The attitudes of the Old Settler faction, the Ridge Faction, and the Treaty Party manifested themselves in bloodshed from time to time. The Creeks had similar circumstances, with the divisions here split along the (old) lines of upper and lower towns. This resembled the Creek Civil War of 1813-14 in Alabama and Georgia as far as factionalism were concerned. This didn't start out initially as a civil conflict. It was precipitated by an attack on a peaceful Tallassee Creek trading party that had left Pensacola and was heading back to its town. The members were attacked at Burnt Corn Creek Alabama on July 27, 1813, by a group of whites commanded by Colonel James Caller of the Alabama militia. As things escalated over a course of months, Andrew Jackson played upon factionalism, and the hostilities took on such tones as to have Creeks fighting against Creeks, sometimes with aid from whites and Cherokees. The Creeks would have the misfortune of seeing their problems erupt into violence at intervals until 1907. While there were specific distinctions among each nation, hostility was a common denominator and hard feelings would continue to smoulder. Albert Pike, an envoy for the south, was to find a receptive ear among some and hesitant audiences elsewhere. Pike was to have little trouble recruiting the loyalty from the elite factions of the societies he approached. Pike was aware of the factionalism that existed within these communities, and he knew where to find receptive audiences that would prove beneficial to the cause of the Confederate States of America. He would move quickly to insure that conditions would favor the South in as quick amount of time as possible. Having a strong presence in Indian Territory was not lost on Pike, nor to those who viewed the importance of Indian Territory as crucial. Between July and October of 1861, treaties would be negotiated with representatives of the "Five Civilized Tribes", as well as relocated Seneca, Quapaw, Osage, Shawnee, Wichita, and Comanche. Hearing promises that would be kept by the C.S.A. as opposed to the U.S.A (which, as of that point in time, had a poor record living up to the promises made to the nations of Indian Territory), the elite of these respective nations realized it was beneficial to take sides, and that side was with the South. Yet among the Traditionalists (the culturally conservative), there was no love for the south. It was white southerners who had forced them out of the homelands of the southeast. Many were old enough to remember their respective "Trail of Tears" where many friends and family members died horrible deaths due to starvation, disease, or exposure to the elements, as many froze to death on the forced journey to Indian Territory. Younger people had heard stories from elders of being forced from homes at bayonet point. Even among those who were not literate by white standards, they were aware that laws had been passed that had proven detrimental to their people. If there were those among the Traditionalists who wanted no part of the United States, they certainly were not about to side with those who had directly oppressed them, now incarnate in the form of the Confederate States of America. As for those who would come to side with the south, there was already animosity toward this elite faction encompassing many issues. These were the ones (in Traditionalists' eyes) who had forsaken their roots. There were some, like Cherokee leader John Ross, who really favored neutrality, yet reluctantly would first side with the C.S.A. By 1861, factionalism among the Cherokees was once again widening. The governing body led by Ross met to try and find the best way to deal with the growing crises. This was done during a time when it was apparent that the Confederate States of America had begun to recruit and mobilize warriors from different factions of Indian Territory. The stage was set among the Cherokee for further internal conflicts, as longtime Ross adversary Stan Watie (eventually) became a confederate brigadier general, the only Native American fighting for the Confederacy to rise to this status. Watie, known by the traditional name of Degataga (the Immovable), had been a longtime member of the Ridge Faction. Members of this faction had signed documents back in the southeast, surrendering vast portions of Cherokee homelands. This was not lost on other Cherokees, and after the forced relocations, bloodshed occurred on numerous occasions. In the years leading up to the civil war, Watie himself had often been a figure in the bloody conflicts that existed in the Cherokee Nation. He was to lead the First Cherokee Regiment, a unit that reportedly saw more action in the western theater of operations during the civil war than any other unit of the Confederate Army. As the unit commander, his unit(s) would see many battles and forays throughout Indian Territory. At one point during the war, Waties' warriors would destroy the Cherokee capital of Talequah, in the process, destroying the home of John Ross as well. As the situation in Indian Territory deteriorated toward war, some would attempt to leave the region altogether. Opthole Yahola, a Creek leader led an exodus toward Kansas as the winter of 1861 descended. Opothole Yahola was no friend of southern interests. On July 10, 1861 some representatives from the Creek Nation signed a treaty with the Confederate States of America. This act fanned the flames of fires that had continued to smoulder along the factional line(s) of the upper and lower towns. It seems that the representatives that signed on the behalf of the Creeks were from lower towns.

By August 5,1861, other members of the Creek Nation's governing body declared those who had signed the treaty had violated tribal law, forfeiting their rights as members of the governing body and were, as a result ousted from the nation. Those who implemented this action were primarily from upper towns. Representatives of the faction who had taken this action left for Washington, D.C. to state their position to the government of the United States. This journey led the representatives first through Kansas. Indian Territory had the misfortune of having pro-C.S.A. Arkansas to the east and Texas on its southern border, which was equally loyal to southern interests. This necessitated taking a travel route through Kansas. U.S. representatives in Kansas received this delegation gladly, for they were aware of developments in Indian Territory and saw the need for allies to try and check Confederate moves in the region. The United States, however, could not at the time promise aid beyond Kansas, which was to leave those who were pro-Union and those who had hoped for neutrality in a desperate situation that was to have dire consequences. Opothole Yahola was not the only one attempting to seek aid from the United States. Around the beginning of November of 1861, a delegation comprising of Creeks, Seminoles, and Chickasaws reached Kansas to meet with U.S. officials in order to find out how a mutually beneficial arrangement could be made. While there had been some in Kansas representing the United States who were ready to enlist the aid of these factions from Indian Territory such as Senator James H. Lane, the federal government true to form continually dragged its feet on the issue of readily supporting an alliance with these factions. Lane initially had no respect for black people in particular. His viewpoint was to change. Senator Lane, who himself had led guerilla actions in the Kansas-Arkansas area with troops of various racial/ethnic backgrounds, was one of the few voices stressing the urgency of having an armed force in Indian Territory loyal to Union interests. The strategic significance of Indian Territory was not lost on Senator Lane and a handful of officials in Kansas. By the time any substantial actions were taken by the United States, the Confederate States of America had close to four thousand warriors from Indian Territory ready to fight on their behalf. Some of the units included the First Cherokee Regiment under Stan Watie, the First Choctaw-Chickasaw Regiment commanded by Major O.G. Welch, the First Cherokee Mounted Rifles commanded by Colonel John Drew, the Cherokee Second Cavalry Regiment under Colonel William Penn Adair, and the Creek First Cavalry Regiment under Colonel D.N. McIntosh.

By the beginning of November in 1861, the refugees traveling with Opothole Yahola consisted of Creeks, but there were also Seminoles, Cherokees, Chickasaws, Yuchis, Caddoes, Quapaws, Witchitas, and Delawares. One of the members of this gathering included Billy Bowlegs. He was the last Seminole leader with his band to be removed from Florida in 1858. It is believed that in Opotole Yahola's entourage, there were about two thousand men.

In all, there were more, as this procession included women, children, and elders of both genders. There were reportedly about three hundred people of African descent among the group. Poorly outfitted, many were to die on the trail, as they not only had to contend with the elements, but with the relentless pursuit of the Choctaw-Chickasaw Regiment and the Cherokee Mounted Rifles. The first of three battles was fought on the night of November 19, 1861, near Round Mountain. Opothole Yahola and the men in the group managed to hold off warriors under the command of Colonel D.H. Cooper. Cooper had a force of fourteen hundred warriors, all of whom were from Indian Territory, with the exception of a small contingent of (white) Texas cavalry. The refugees managed to escape to the territory of friendly Cherokees. Cooper's men didn't press the pursuit at this point, as he had received other orders. Cooper and his men next engaged these refugees at Bird Creek on December 9th. Opothole Yahola here had been joined by a sizable contingent of (four companies) of sympathetic Cherokees commanded by Colonel John Drew. Again, the refugees were able to escape as a result of the aid received from the Cherokees and the courage of the men in the entourage. Colonel Cooper faced a dilemma in that some of his warriors might defect to Drew. Thus, he was hesitant to press a close pursuit again. The engagement fought on the afternoon of December 26, 1861, was a different matter altogether. The Battle of Chustenahlah left the refugees devastated as they succumbed to warriors under the command of Colonel James McIntosh. The men of the refugees had gallantly fought with their pursuers on two previous occasions. The third time was not to be in their favor.

These men held off McIntosh's warriors as long as they could, giving time for their companions to keep up the flight toward Kansas. Some of those of African descent who were captured alive would end up being sold to the highest bidder. One hundred sixty women and children were captured by McIntosh's men. The intensity of the Battle of Chustenahlah had forced the refugees to leave behind the possessions they had with them. The material possessions some had carried from their homes in Indian Territory had fallen into the hands of their opposition. The refugees who had survived the perilous journey came into Kansas in motley groups. Once in Kansas, the survivors would be joined by the refugees who had fled there in smaller groups prior to Opothole Yahola's journey. As the survivors continued to drift in, they were truly a pathetic sight to behold. All were destitute. As it was now winter, the fact that these men, women, and children survived was a testimony to their strength. Many had died along the way during the tribulations of the exodus. Those representatives of the United States who were in Kansas now became soberly aware of the threat now existing in Indian Territory. Institutions of the United States were slow in responding to the welfare of the refugees, and even then, the response was inadequate. Decent food was in short supply. Shelter where it did exist was poor at best. As well as intentions may have been, it was impossible to provide adequate medical attention to the refugees. By the time all refugees fleeing Indian Territory would straggle in, their numbers exceeded seven thousand. Opothole Yahola and his daughter were among the many victims of circumstance to die in the refugee camps. There were instances of women giving birth in the snow, with no shelter and no clothing for their newborns. Because of the large numbers of frostbitten victims, amputation became one of the most common medical procedures throughout the camps.

In the aftermath of the flight of Opothole Yahola and his intertribal refugees, there were now a large number of men willing to fight. Indeed, these survivors of the exodus from Indian Territory into Kansas had already seen combat during their trip north, as they had been forced to fight pursuing Confederate Army units that trailed them almost the entire length of the journey. Some of the Seminole and Creek men were old enough to remember their own war experiences back in the pinelands and swamps of Alabama, Georgia, and Florida. Exiled Creeks, Cherokees, Seminoles, Yuchis, Chickasaws, Choctaws, Delawares, and Shawnees (among others) would form the nucleus of new combat units. These units were the First Kansas Colored Infantry, Second Kansas Colored Infantry, First Indian Home Guards, Second Indian Home Guards, Third Indian Regiment, The Fifth Indian Home Guard, Second Colored Artillery, Fifty-Sixth Colored Infantry, and the Sixtieth Colored Infantry. And as time went on, the ranks of the refugees overall would continue to grow. Back in Indian Territory, there were instances where culturally conservative Cherokees who became known as "pins" would liberate and ally themselves with Africans in order to fight against Confederate units. During the civil war, it was not unusual to hear of slaveholders complaining that male slaves in particular were escaping with increased frequency. Some of these men would eventually find themselves in Union colors, fighting against the forces of the Confederacy. One such man by the name of

Charley Nave had been a slave in the Cherokee Nation. He would see combat at Honey Springs and after the war, serve five years as a member of the Tenth Cavalry. The designation of the term "Pins" would come to be used decades later during both the Green Peach War (Ispachar's War) and the Crazy Snake Wars to designate culturally conservative Creeks. And while there has been a focus on what certain segments of the five nations (the elite class) of the southeast did socially to people of African descent with the implementation of chattel slavery, it can be stated that there were factions within the nations that felt chattel slavery was against the ways of the people. The "pins" reflected this value as they remained loyal to the ancestral vision that saw life through a more humanitarian focus. There was the realization that there was a commonality that was shared as far as adversity was concerned. There were communities back in the east that were remote in terms of location to white settlements. The populations in these areas consisted of people that had African ancestry and now lived their lives within the boundaries of Cherokee territory. Those who were born Cherokee and lived in proximity to these areas tended to be Traditionalists. The pins were also realists, as they knew those that were freed from their situation would be willing to fight back if given the opportunity. And while units that were formed in Kansas were comprised of men who were representative of what the populations of their communities looked liked, the U.S. Army formulated and tried to assemble the units based on the racial attitudes of the period. Some of the units were supposedly all "colored". Others were all "Indian". An interesting dynamic played out once again where there were instances when the white command structure could not communicate verbally with native soldiers. Again, the skills of men of African descent (some of mixed African-Native ancestry) aware of a respective culture because of life experience, served as translators due to their multilingual abilities. By the conclusion of the civil war, these units would distinguish themselves in their respective theater of war, often fighting against not only white Confederate units, but native ones as well. As in the United States, brother would fight brother, and former slave would engage in combat with former slave owner.

Some of the male refugees were to form the nucleus of fighting forces that would see combat in the region. Units such as the First and Second Kansas Colored of the United States Colored Troops were formed, along with the with the First, Second and Third Indian Home Guard Regiments. Here old roles were again played out as those of African descent among the troops acted as translators, since many of them spoke English as well as the indigenous language of their home communities. There were some older black Seminoles that had seen combat in Florida. Over the course of the war, warriors from all factions would continually clash in some of the most integrated battles of the conflict. These battles were to scar Indian Territory deeply. The Battle of Honey Springs in the Creek Nation took place on July 17, 1863. Elements of Union forces learned that units of the Confederacy were going to attempt to take Fort Gibson in Kansas. Large numbers of Confederate troops (of varying skin complexions) were seen advancing toward Honey Springs. Enslaved Africans that were in the vicinity of

Honey Springs related of how gunfire was heard in the distance. Those people in the immediate area who had Confederate sympathies decided to take cover as best they could and abandoned their lands to find shelter in the surrounding woods. Sounds of battle continued all day and into the night. Later, many Confederate soldiers were witnessed fleeing away from the seen as the Union forces turned the tide of the battle and gained the upper hand in the confrontation. Some Union units had already forced an advanced guard of the Confederacy to fall back toward Honey Springs on the night of July 15th. By the actual time of the battle, it could have been characterized in contemporary terms as affirmative action in overtime. Men of African descent, as well as Native Americans and whites on both sides were involved in this fight. Units reportedly involved were (for the Union) the First Kansas Colored, First and Second Indian Regiments, the Sixth Kansas Cavalry, and the 2nd Colorado Infantry.

For the Confederacy there were two Creek Regiments, two Cherokee Regiments commanded by Stan Watie, the Fifth Texas Partisans, the Twenty-Ninth Texas Cavalry, with reserve units of the Choctaw- Chickasaw Regiment and two squadrons of Texas Cavalry in reserve. These units were supported by an artillery battery consisting of four cannons. After an artillery duel, the First Kansas Colored and the Second Indian Regiment broke the Confederate line at Elk Creek. This was crucial, as it turned the tide of battle in favor of the Union forces. The Confederate retreat was covered by intense fire laid down by the Choctaw-Chickasaw Regiment and the Texas Cavalry that had been held in reserve. Union Cavalry units found this out as they attempted to pursue some of the retreating Confederate troops. Stan Watie would gain fame as his units perfected and effectively applied hit-and-run guerilla tactics. Units under his command were believed to have seen the most combat in the western theater. Watie was also the last Confederate general to acknowledge the victory of the United States when he surrendered on June 21, 1865. Indian Territory was not the only theater of action for warriors of color. For the Union, in the east were units of the First Michigan Sharpshooters, Company K, which had one hundred Ottawas as part of the unit. Company D of the Fourteenth New York Artillery had eight Senecas from Cattaraugas, New York. Some indigenous men were placed in units of the United States Colored Troops if they didn't look "Indian" enough. Austin George, a Mashantucket Pequot from Connecticut, and Private Clinton Mountpleasant of Lewiston, New York, who was Iroquois, were only two examples of these kinds of occurrences. These men were placed in the Thirty-First United States Colored Troops. After 1863, there was a concerted effort to recruit men of African descent into the United States armed forces. They would be in segregated units commanded by white officers. The Fifty-Fourth Massachusetts has been the subject of various studies. It is conceivable that some of these men had indigenous ancestry as well. On the Confederate side were units such as the Fifth, Twelfth, and Seventeenth South Carolina Infantry who had a number of Catawba Men in their ranks. These were in addition to Confederate units active in and around "Indian Territory".

During the civil war, some of those with Confederate sympathies fled into

Texas, taking whatever they could with them. This included, in many instances, their slaves. After the war, there were to be migrations of this refugees back into Indian Territory in the attempt to pick up their lives. Those who had been enslaved for the most part also journeyed back to Indian Territory. Those who did not do so immediately struck out and took their chances in "America". Many of these people would shortly realize they would be better off rebuilding their lives in Indian Territory, and headed back. In spite of the fact of being former slaves, many of these people had culturally retained customs and traits of the nations in which they had lived in. There would also be large numbers of those who were formerly enslaved who would journey to Indian Territory, as it was believed to be a better chance of a decent life minus the hypocritic trappings of attempting to live in the United States. Some of these people would continue to journey westward, bypassing Indian Territory altogether. The conclusion of the war had its share of ironies. It is said that at the surrender at Appomattox Virginia, Robert E. Lee mistook Ely Parker, a Seneca and an officer on the staff of Ulysses S. Grant, for a black man. Until the identification of General Parker was confirmed, Lee took offense as to the presence of this man.

War is a horrible situation. As people started back to areas to begin the long laborious task of putting their lives back together, there was another slap in the face. It was convenient to exploit the position of the war weary to one's own advantage. After the civil war, the United States Government was the entity looking to get what it could. The United States Government used the fact that some indigenous people had fought for the Confederacy as an excuse to take what they could from the nations that the warriors came from. This happened regardless of the fact that there were many indigenous men who had fought bravely while wearing the uniform of the United States. This was not a new situation; the United States had taken similar actions against the Iroquois Confederacy after the War of Independence. Even though some Iroquois warriors had fought for the United States, all were subject to having their lands taken after the signing of the Treaty of 1783. With this as a backdrop, the peoples of Indian Territory again faced the job of rebuilding their farms, schools, and churches, as well as various institutions that were damaged or destroyed during the years of martial upheaval. There was certainly a history of responding to turmoil, and the people(s) would rise again to meet the challenges once more set before them.

As the nations began to rebound from the effects of war, businesses of all kinds established or re-established themselves. Members of the different nations became prosperous through these various business endeavors, as well as through the leasing of different areas of land in the respective nations, taking advantage of resources like coal and timber. As things progressed, some of African descent living in the territory would prosper in many instances, as numerous business endeavors were to pay off after the input of hard work. While there were instances of social adversity, those residing in Indian Territory faced the prospect of better living conditions than those of African descent living in white America. During the earlier years of colonization, which were followed by the establishment of the United States, many of African descent fled to indigenous communities in the hopes of finding a better life. This covered the timeframe from the 1500s to the early 1800s. After the forced removal of many indigenous people to Indian Territory which began in the 1830s, there was a new social climate forming. It is rare to hear of people of African descent running to Indian Territory in the years leading up to the civil war. After the war, this changed to an extent. In some instances, there were those who were traveling west to seek what they could, and not necessarily having Indian Territory as a destination in mind. Others specifically looked to try and integrate into the existing communities, some of which had predominately black settlements. Some of these towns were comprised of former slaves and/or people of African-Native ancestry. These settlements existed and continued to exist (until statehood in 1907) as part of a respective nation. There were towns established that could trace their roots to settlements that came into existence after the forced removals from the southeast. These had colorful backgrounds. Wewoka (in the Seminole Nation) was founded by John Horse. The towns of North Fork and Canadian Colored were in the Creek Nation. Long- established residents of the territory distinguished themselves from new migrants to the region. The term "State Negroes" was used by their "Indian" counterparts. Others were to become (especially as the twentieth century dawned) non affiliated with any indigenous nation. This was in a climate that saw whites as well, squatting on lands as opportunity presented itself.

Full citizenship had come to the people of African descent who had roots among the Seminole and Creek Nations after the war. Some of the Seminoles had occupied prominent positions prior to the war. Representatives of the Dosar Barkus Band and Caesar Brunner Band were to sit on the council of the Seminole Nation until July of 2000 (Caesar Brunner had been an interpreter, his services utilized in particular in negotiations with the United States in the months after the civil war). There were some in the Creek Nation who would serve in the two primary governing bodies, the House of Kings and the House of Warriors. Eventually the Cherokee Nation granted citizenship to those of African descent who were former slaves or Freedmen who had resided in the nation prior to the war. There were to be issues that would arise that challenged the status of citizens within respective nations. In 1883 there was the question of how the Cherokee Nation of Oklahoma would allocate three hundred thousand dollars in federal money that had been allocated to the Cherokee National Council. Dennis Bushyhead, Principal Chief from 1879 to 1887, was one leader who had the interest of the various factions of the community at heart, including the status of the Freedmen. Some factions on the National Council thought otherwise. After a series of legal actions that would bring in the United States Government, all of the factions entitled to a share of the money in question received their share. The Choctaws and Chickasaws were the longest holdouts as far as granting citizenship. This status of citizenship would elude the Chickasaw Freedmen. Yet among many of the everyday people, social integration was a fact of life, despite what was happening on the political level. Among the Traditionalists (the culturally conservative), those of African descent found more acceptance, and in many instances, these community members would largely adopt or had already adopted for whatever length of time the attitudes and values of their neighbors.

While there would continue to be numerous issues that needed to be addressed throughout the Territory, the vast majority of citizens were honest, hardworking people. Yet there was a criminal element. Indian Territory was a large area with varied terrain, ranging from the mountains to prairie to desert. In this area, there were limitless locations that offered sanctuary for those on the run. The Territory would see the rise of outlaws of all colors who used the area as a refuge while carrying on their nefarious trade in the area and surrounding states. This, in turn, led to the rise of lawmen. Some of these institutions had existed from the beginnings of the nations in the Territory. The LightHorse was a good example of this. Each nation, be they Seminole, Creek, Cherokee, Choctaw, or Chickasaw, had its own court system. These were located in the capitals and/or major towns of the respective nations. Tishomingo (Chickasaw), Wewoka (Seminole), Talequah (Cherokee), Ockmulgee (Creek), and Tuskahoma (Choctaw) were some of the primary locations for these courts. Other situations were to happen after the civil war, such as the stationing of the U.S. Marshals. Because of racism, LightHorse officers could only arrest red and black offenders. If a native offender was in the company of a white outlaw, he could not be arrested by a LightHorse officer. This fell under the jurisdiction of the U.S. Marshals. There were never more than two hundred deputies to patrol an area of seventy- four thousand square miles. The exploits and adventures of these good and bad guys are of epic proportions, and unfortunately, many of these stories have not found their way to mainstream culture. Nevertheless, all of the elements of adventure were to stay present in the territory. These were to exist for decades as outlaws and lawmen plied back and forth. Out of necessity, the lawmen were of all colors. Many were already residents of the nations. It was a definite advantage to be familiar with the country and be from the culture(s) of the region, as journeys were to take lawmen over vast distances. Being able to handle oneself in combat, be it gunplay or hand-to-hand, was also a requisite. The lawmen, be they LightHorse or Marshal had to be good trackers, as they often had to follow a trail that had gone cold. Being able to recognize signs while on the trail was also a way to stay ahead of an outlaw or outlaws. Out on the trail, there were few, if any, witnesses, and ambushes were not unheard of. The kinds of skills previously mentioned added insurance of not only capturing and delivering prisoners, but staying alive in the first place. The outlaws generally had a few things in their favor. The terrain was such that escape and evasion was easy. Detecting oncoming lawmen was not difficult. Names like the Rufus Buck Gang, Cherokee Bill, Dick Glass, Isom Dart, and George Lanre are only a few of the names that commanded respect because of their bad reputations revolving around any number of criminal activities. But names like Bass Reeves, Sam Sixkiller, Grant Johnson, and Zeke Miller are among the many names of lawmen who stood in the way of those who had nefarious activities on their minds. By 1875, the federal judge overseeing the administration of law on the federal level was Issac Charles Parker, who was to become known as the "Hanging Judge Parker". Yet not all of the violent activity was criminal in nature. Two Cherokee cattlemen, John and

Dick Vann, and members of the Creek LightHorse had gunfights in December of 1878 and August of 1879, the latter encounter ending up with fatalities. These incidents happened near Marshall Town in the Creek Nation. It so happens that the LightHorse officers involved were of African/Creek ancestry. During the August 1879 incident, John Vann was killed.

Thus, during the time period after the civil war, Indian Territory continued to undergo a process of evolving. There was no such thing as utopia. There were certainly pluses and minuses about the situation(s), yet the communities proceeded with the course of life. Ruling tribal governments would legislate one thing, but the reality was not absolute by any stretch of the imagination, as people went about living their lives adhering, in some instances, to culturally conservative values. These values were at times at odds with the ruling councils. Many of the nations were, in fact, rainbow nations in that the residents and citizens were of varying ethnic backgrounds. And while this multiethnicity was a fact, there were citizens who soley considered themselves Creek, Seminole, Cherokee, etc. in spite of ongoing sociopolitical stresses. For example, one lawman who gained repute, Deputy U.S. Marshal Bass Reeves, once stated that he knew if he had to go after a Seminole, he faced the fact that Seminoles stuck together. Yet the expansionist goals of the United States again penetrated to reek their own kind of havoc. By the 1870s and 80s, squatters had staked their claim in many areas of Indian Territory and adjacent lands, such as those located in Kansas. The region in general stood on the verge of a wave of massive influxes of people seeking to establish a better life for themselves. They were different from the people who had migrated to the region after the civil war to become part of a respective nation (regardless of their status, these people, to whatever degree, acknowledged the sovereignty of their host nation). Yet the newcomers often didn't care about the communities where they were setting down ties. At times, units of the U.S Army were needed to quell unrest around the phenomenon of large groups of outsiders inundating an area. This was increasingly the case as the 1880s progressed, as people were steadily seeking what was felt to be opportunities, and in larger and larger numbers, occupiying regions of Indian Territory. At times, situations threatened to escalate into violence. Units of the Tenth Calvary, (Buffalo Soldiers) were among the military units that responded to various incidents.

While this was happening, (white) business interests of the times had already had numerous dealings with tribal councils around a number of issues that affected their business pursuits. Railroad companies had to negotiate terms of agreement in order to navigate their lines through Indian Territory. The cattle industry played a large part of the picture as many drives would take place using routes from Texas into Indian Territory where rail lines were located. Many men were to find work in this rough and dangerous profession. The land itself was valuable, as it was leased to railroad companies and cattlemen looking to drive their herds to market (cattle ranching remains a prominent, economic venture for some native communities today). Meat companies were in a similar situation in that herds of cattle had to be moved from southern areas such as Texas to the railroad lines running through Indian Territory. Thus, agreements needed to be reached at times with nations located in the territory, to insure as best as possible the movement of cattle to the railroad lines (not to mention taking into account the many hazards of moving massive heads of cattle several hundred miles). Some of the nations negotiated terms of land usages, guaranteeing additional sources of income into their respective treasuries. In moving cattle herds through the territory payments required that the method would be in money and/or beef. Whenever possible, those who led the cattle drives attempted to move the herds through less-populated areas of Indian Territory to avoid paying any kind of fee(s). This often meant moving the herds through the more western extremes of the territory. Reports from the cattlemen mentioned time and time again that many settlements they moved their respective herds through were, at times, black towns. As some of the nations of the territory were racially mixed, this is no surprise. Driving cattle is hard, dangerous work. In the best of worlds, there were many hazards. To attempt moving large herds north, away from any settlements, increased the risk of having some of the cattle stolen. The complexion of the thieves could vary. The ironic twist of fate in this situation was that the expansion of rail lines was (along with other factors) responsible for the near extermination of the great bison herds of the plains. Railroad companies hired hunters to shoot the animals, which numbered in the millions. One result was the near destruction of many of the cultures of the Great Plains, which had at their spiritual base this massive mammal. Certainly, the turmoil and upheaval created by the killing of the bison, coinciding with the military actions of the United States Army in its various incarnations, came close enough in wiping the cultures of the Plains. Hundreds of cultures east of the Mississippi River had been in contact with different European entities for centuries. With the formation of the United States, the tide of expansion steamrolled. Indigenous cultures were seen as a hinderance to progress, and by and large, the wellbeing of these nations was not a priority or concern. It was now the time of the Plains people, as well as the cultures located along the Pacific Coast, to suffer as a result of the tide of expansion. The native peoples of California and some parts of the southwest and northwest had already been witness to encroachment, first from the Spanish, the Russians, the British, and then from the United States. What was initially a trickle with the journeys of Alexander Mackenzie in 1793, the Lewis and Clark Expedition of 1804, and various agents of the expanding fur trade that swept across the continent and into the Rocky Mountains by land and water between 1800 and the 20's, was now a flood. Cheyenne, Arapaho, Lakota, Nakota, Dakota, Comanche, and Crow, among others, used bison for nearly all of their food and material needs. Decline of the herds meant that the days of the Plains culture were in serious jeopardy. As these nations were forced onto reservations, their lands were taken. In actuality, the lands had been the victims of encroachment for some time. Armed resistance was determined, and the reaction of the various Plains people and their respective warrior societies was an effort that any sovereign nation would take when threatened. Many nations in what is now the eastern United States had also put up armed resistance, as well as diplomatic efforts, in attempts

to ward off the steady encroachment on their sovereignty. The last of these uprisings, the brief Ute War of 1915 and the Battle at Bear Valley Arizona, involving
thirty Yaqui men (this occurred in 1918 with Troop E of the Tenth Cavalry
involved), ended with unconfirmed reports of some of these men being sold into
slavery in Central America.

One direct result of the end of the civil war was that now the full resources
of the United States military machine could now be focused on subjugating peoples of the northern, southern, and central plains, as well as those living along the
west coast and adjacent areas. Despite the fact that there had been numerous
slave revolts over a long period of time, conflicts such as the Seminole War (the
first and second outbreak of hostilities in particular), and even the War of
Independence, also called the American Revolution, there was an attitude and
prevailing disposition on the behalf of many white Americans that black men
were poor soldiers. Long gone was the memory of the fact that at various times
during the colonial era, enslaved Africans would be given arms to fight on the
side of their oppressors, against whatever foe. And while the governing class had
reservations when it came time to disarming these men (the fear of armed insur-
rection was a concern, and records show time and time again that more daring
men would not hesitate to strike back if possible), when things came to a crisis
point, black men were given arms. The U.S. Military realized that during the
early years of the civil war, the Union was in serious trouble and would have to
explore whatever options were available in order to combat the military machine
of the Confederacy. By the end of the war, units such as the Louisiana Native
Guards (the first unit of soldiers of African descent to exist officially in the
United States military), Fifty-Fourth and Fifty-Fifth and Massachusetts, The
First and Second Kansas Colored, and the Indian Home Guards, among many
others, proved (once again) that there was no question of fighting ability of black
troops. Not only had combat skills come to be valued, but in some instances,
those who were either of mixed African-Native heritage or culturally part of a
specific nation (i.e. Creek, Seminole) served as interpreters. Many of these men
were multilingual, speaking native language(s) as well as English. The units that
were serving often were comprised of men who spoke only their native language.
As some of the the First Kansas Colored had the distinction of being among the
first units with men of African descent to see combat in the war in 1862. They
also had the distinction of sharing with black units that were present at Fort
Pillow Tennessee, at having some of the worst atrocities of the war happening to
them as the majority of the unit was massacred at Poison Springs, Arkansas, in
April of 1864. With the conclusion of the civil war, the eyes of white expansion
once again focused westward. In order to insure the tide would flow west, it was
determined that additional measures were to be implemented. It was a fact that
many of the nations of the Plains and other western areas were militarily formidable. The Lakotas, under Red Cloud, for example, had to back up his words and
eventually, because of the actions taken by warriors of his people, they were able
to bring the U.S. Army to the negotiating table. The events that was to lead various bands of Teton Lakotas (of which Red Cloud was one) taking to the warpath

can be traced to a location in Wyoming that was at one time a trading post that was purchased and transformed by the United States Army. With the arrival of white soldiers at Fort Laramie, peoples of the area such as the Lakotas, Cheyenne, and Arapahoes began to take offense to the incursion. To add to this, in 1862, an explorer named John Bozeman had established a route that began in Wyoming and went through Montana. In doing this, the travel time into locations of the northwest was shortened. This meant however that travelers were journeying through the heart of territory utilized by the Teton Lakotas and their allies. This region was no stranger to tensions that erupted into violence. There had been numerous encounters for more than twenty years, which led to lives being lost on both sides. Yet again, the stage was being set for another explosion. Army representatives had desired for years to build additional forts leading to the northwest. There had been attempts at negotiations where the Army had hoped to be able to gain access for travelers along the route that led northwest. Time and time again, native leaders could not accept some of the terms that were presented at the negotiating table. At one meeting, Red Cloud and some of his allies had walked out in disgust. With the establishment of the Bozeman Trail, there had been numerous attempts to gain the upper hand militarily, ideally deceiving the watchful eyes of the different warrior societies of the area. Warriors had successfully closed down the Bozeman Trail, as well as the Oregon Trail at first, attacking travelers who dared to trespass in the territory. But in 1866, the U.S. Army managed to establish or enlarge Forts Reno, Phil Kearney, and C.F. Smith. A Captain William Fetterman contemptuously boasted that he could destroy the entire Lakota Nation with eighty men. Given the knowledge of current events of the time, and the area where Fetterman was, and the longstanding history of the fighting prowess of the various bands of Lakotas, one could question the sanity of this statement made by Captain Fetterman, and how a professional military man would have faith in this false sense of security. On December 21,1866, Fetterman and eighty soldiers would pay for this arrogant naivete when warriors under Red Cloud, killed the entire contingent near Fort Phil Kearney. As in some years before, it was clear there was not to be a military solution (once more) to this issue, at least one the Army would favor. They now had to meet on terms set by the native leaders. Although a temporary reprieve, the Fort Laramie Treaty of 1868 was a result of Lakota determination to cease the onslaught that was beginning to overwhelm the lands upon which they lived. As fate would have it, the years that had led to the signing of the Fort Laramie Treaty of 1868 bore witness to a rising force among the Lakotas. This warrior had already, in numerous encounters over the years, proven his skill in battle. This man was Crazy Horse of the Hunkpitila. U.S. representatives were insistent that there be one individual, one "chief" to speak for the entire nation. Such was the desire here again. True to many native cultures however, while there are strong relations between various bands, autonomy is a fact, one that is deeply respected. Red Cloud represented the interests of his band and, quite possibly, those who were allied with his (band). This had no bearing on other bands of Lakota. The Fort Laramie Treaty, for example, meant nothing to Sitting Bull and his band of Hunkpapas.

The Cheyenne (whose various bands had suffered at the hands of numerous attacks on their camps by whites) had plenty of reasons to be hostile. The Blackfoot Confederacy, and the different bands of Apache, Comanche, and Kiowa, among others, were equally as formidable, and over the years had made it clear through their actions that there would be a price to pay if white encroachment was to be persistent. The United States Government, and specifically, the military establishment, turned to face the situation.

There was a concern, which turned out to be unfounded, of a possible French invasion based in Mexico. If this was to materialize, the southwestern areas such as Texas, New Mexico, and Arizona, might become theaters of combat. The military establishment, specifically the army, turned its attention to the west. To answer the need for manpower to patrol the vast regions of the west, it was determined to utilize black soldiers as part of this strategy. On a subliminal level, given the now centuries-old variety of tactics formulated to foster antagonism, perhaps this was seen by some in the government as a way of having two groups of peoples pitted once more in an adversarial capacity on a level previously not seen in North America. Over the centuries, native men had been used against escaped slaves (some of whom were of mixed black and red bloodlines, as well as some being only of native blood) and maroon settlements (some of which were racially-mixed communities). In some instances slaves, were armed and commanded to destroy native settlements. Throughout what is now the United States, this had occurred. French Louisiana in 1729, and New Amsterdam (New York) from 1641 to 1643 are only two of many instances. This legacy was to again be re-enacted with the full sanction and resources of the United States military machine. By an act of Congress on July 28, 1866, specific legislation called for "an act to increase and fix the military peace establishment of the United States". This would create an additional four cavalry regiments to the six already on active duty, "two of which shall be composed of colored men, having the same organizations is now provided by law for cavalry regiments". Thus the Ninth and Tenth Cavalry had the groundwork laid, which led to their formation. The Buffalo Soldiers were in the embryonic stage. August 3,1866, under the direction of Major General Philip Sheridan, saw the beginning stages of the Ninth Cavalry in New Orleans. Similar measures were undertaken on August 9, 1866 in St. Louis, Missouri by Lieutenant General Sherman, which saw the formation of the Tenth Cavalry. The same Act of July 28, 1866, impacted the infantry. The act called for "eight new regiments of ten companies each, four regiments of which shall be composed of colored men". Another act, the Act of March 3, 1869, would downsize and consolidate the infantry from forty five regiments into twenty five regiments. As a result, what had previously been the Thirty- Eighth and Forty-First Regiments, would now be designated the Twenty-Fourth Infantry, what was previously known as the Thirty- Ninth and Fortieth-Infantry, was now designated the Twenty-Fifth Infantry. As fate would have it, it would be a military delegate from the Twenty- Fifth Infantry who was ordered to proceed to Nacimiento Mexico, and lay the groundwork for the formation of the Seminole Negro Indian Scouts in 1869. This was only one of several Seminole communities located in this region of Mexico. These family groups were, for the most part refugees from the political situation in Indian Territory who had in 1849 and 1850, decided that it was best to relocate elsewhere. By this point in time, the inhabitant of these communities were not all necessarily Seminole, but Creek, Cherokee, and Biloxi, as well as free blacks and escaped slaves who took a chance for freedom by fleeing southward into Mexico. The communities by this time had a distinct composition of people who were of African ancestry, as well as native ancestry in some, although not all, cases. Other settlement locations included Lagunna de Parras (along with Nacimiento, located in the state of Coahuila) Matamoros and Nueces River, Texas. While in Mexico, the warriors of these communities had distinguished themselves in battle on several occasions by assisting the Mexican Government as soldiers in the region. On some occasions, the warriors had to defend their own communities from attack. Some of the men were old enough to remember being involved in the guerilla conflict in the pinelands, sawgrass, and swamps back on the Florida peninsula.

There were some who were younger who did not share this experience. An examination of the first muster roll in 1870 of the Seminole Negro Indian Scouts shows the ages of these men ranged from eighteen to sixty. Yet by the time they were approached by representatives from the United States Army, there was no question as to their prowess as fighting men. Their skills as far as relating to the environment were equal to their skills in combat. Time and time again, during their existence, the almost uncanny ability to track adversaries through terrain that seemed untrackable and their physical endurance in environments that were considered hostile by some, would earn the praise (sometimes unwillingly) of the Army brass, not to mention their commanders in the field. The time period of the mid and late nineteenth century would have these units aid travelers like wagon trains heading westward, police illegal squatters in Indian Territory, and guard areas under construction, such as railroads. The Ninth and Tenth Cavalry both were part of the charge up San Juan Hill in Cuba during the Spanish American War. Some units would pursue followers of the Mexican revolutionary Pancho Villa into Mexico in 1916. These soldiers would do this and more. Yet the tasks that would gain them the most prominence was the fact that they would see combat against numerous groups of Native American peoples ranging from the north to the southern Plains (and, in some instances, the mountains of the southwest) for the rest of the nineteenth century.

Although the Buffalo Soldiers are known primarily as soldiers who fought against native peoples, this was not always the case. As in other parts of the United States, there had been numerous clashes between native peoples of Colorado and white settlers. To say the least, there were more than sufficient grounds for suspicion and apprehension. The horrors of Sand Creek in 1864, when Black Kettle's band of Cheyennes were attacked while Black Kettle waved an American Flag in the face of charging Colorado militia (in an attempt to show his people's peaceful intentions) led by John Chivington, stands out as the most infamous. There were reports that there were whites who were in the village at the time that were killed during the attack. Violence was not a new occurrence in this region.

Confrontations between the Utes and whites in the region began in 1859. Ouray, a Ute Chief, attempted in the 1860s and early 1870s to hold together a fragile truce through his diplomatic efforts. As time passed, more and more, it became evident that the Utes were the ones on the losing side, as more and more of the lands that had been under their custodianship slipped away. Peace was not to be lasting. In 1887, Colorow, a Comanche (captured as a child), who had been raised among the Ute and risen to leadership among the White River Utes, led some of his people away from a reservation in Utah, bound for traditional grounds in Colorado. His band was pursued by a posse led by a sheriff who was intent on arresting Colorow for stealing horses. When the posse caught up with Colorow, he denied having any part in this instance of horse theft. A gunfight started, but Colorow wasn't taken into custody. Members of this posse a short time later re-entered the camp of Colorow when Colorow and his men were away, terrorizing the women and children occupants, engaging in arson, vandalism, and their own horse thefts. Colorow, upon returning, realized things were only going to get worse and quickly began to move his people back to the Utah reservation in the hopes of avoiding further trouble. Colorow's fears were justified. The governor of Colorado at the time, Alva Adams, had ordered the state militia to overtake Colorow's band before they could return to Utah. Given the fierce anti-native sentiments present among some government officials and segments of Colorado's white population at the time, it can be speculated where the outcome of an encounter may have led. Before this could happen Lieutenant George Burnett of the 9th Cavalry, (a white officer) stationed at Fort Duchesne, Utah, caught wind of the events and, with ten troopers of the Ninth Cavalry, raced to meet Colorow's band and escort them safely back to the reservation in Utah. Although numerically small, the militia, and the posse with its components, a cross- section of characters who were to be found in frontier communities of the time, realized it would be nothing but more trouble than they could bargain for if they attacked anyone under the protection of the U.S. Army, regardless of what color the soldiers were. As a result of this action, initial apprehensions toward the Ninth Cavalry that had existed on the behalf of the Ute people in the area were greatly reduced. As word of this event spread, the Ute people of the area came to trust and respect the troops of this unit of the Ninth.

It can be said that in warfare, the term being-in the wrong place at the wrong time is tragically enacted. In war, some live while others die. Isaiah Dorman was of African ancestry. He had familiarity with areas of the west and knew his way around the backcountry. During this time, he learned the ways of some of the Plains people, one of which was language acquisition. It is said that he preferred the company of northern Plains people and had come to be admired and respected by the Lakotas. His wife was Santee of Inkpaduta's band. He would earn money by wood cutting, being a mail courier, and being a guide. His bilingual skill was seen as a plus to the U.S. Army that patrolled the region of the northern Plains known as the Dakota Territory. As of 1871, he was hired as an interpreter at the Army's Fort Rice. He was unfortunately a scout with the Seventh

Cavalry in 1875, a situation that would lead to his fate of being mortally wounded at the Battle of the Greasy Grass, more commonly known as the Battle of the Little Bighorn, where George Armstrong Custer finally met his match, taking more than two hundred soldiers of his immediate command to death with him. Dorman was with the units of cavalry commanded by Major Marcus Reno when the actual battle began. When Tatanka Iantanka (Sitting Bull) was told of a "wasicum sapa" (white man, black) lying on the battlefield, he rushed to the scene to be horrified that it was a man he considered a friend. After giving Isaiah Dorman a requested drink of water, Sitting Bull witnessed the death of his friend.

But in the end, an era of change was happening, and as it was for the nations of the east, it was negative changes for most of the Plains people. The nations of Indian Territory managed for some time to ward off this predation, and work the situation to the advantage of their respective people, although there were still more culturally conservative factions that held onto the old ways as best they could and frowned on these kind of endeavors undertaken by their governing councils. Yet regardless of what laws were passed, it is a mistake to view legislative measures of the day to the realities within segments of communities. Back in Indian Territory, the end of national sovereignty was nearing. With the implementation of the General Allotment (Dawes) Act of 1887, it may have seemed (on the surface) that there were those in the federal government who really had the best interest of native people in mind. The reality, however, was quite different. This was yet another assimilation attempt that would undermine the autonomy and gains that had been made in the territory in the time period when most of these relocated nations had occupied the area. The thirty- six nations of the territory, many of which had been forcefully relocated to the area during different times in the 1830s, were again about to experience the impact of legislative onslaught. This act of federal legislation would allot (in its initial form) one hundred sixty acres of land to the head of a household. This was a continuation in the endeavor to convert many to strictly agricultural pursuits. A census was to be initiated that was to supposedly determine who belonged to what nation. In allotting the land, tribal governments were to be abolished. This also meant the land base of a given nation would be seriously undermined, if not eradicated altogether. The implication was that a nation would cease to exist as a sovereign entity. Under the original act, governments of the Chickasaw, Creek, Choctaw, Cherokee, Seminole, Seneca, Kaws, Quapaws, Confederated Peorias, and Osage were not to be affected. These nations had negotiated terms that were to allow them to continue with a certain degree of autonomy (as best could be under the circumstances). There were to be several modifications to the Dawes Act. Each of the modifications infringed on the benefits that any native person hoped to realize under the legislation. One of the results was the reduction in the size of allotment from the original one hundred sixty acres to eighty acres. Over one hundred million acres of land once overseen by numerous native nations would be under control of entities outside of their respective communities when the terms of the Dawes Act concluded in 1930. The Commissioner of Indian Affairs was now authorized to lease some of the original lands to white people (those who were not residents of a specific indigenous nation). The mid and late 1880s had seen a rush of outsiders inundating lands of the territory. By the last part of the century, (the 1890s), there was increasingly outside commercial interests who eyed the lands for places to set up their endeavors. By the early 1890s, coal veins were found in different nations of the territory. Eventually, oil would be found in other areas in the early years of the twentieth century. There continued to be the ongoing issue of the competence of a native person(s) to handle his/her own business affairs. The question of competency was determined by representatives of the Bureau of Indian Affairs. The Curtis Act of 1898 gave authorization to the Dawes Commission to allot land to members of the "Five Civilized Tribes" and abolish their governments. In the hopes of maintaining some kind of autonomy, the respective tribal governments entered into discussions with the Commission trying to salvage what they could. As a result of the negotiations, by 1897, the tribal governments reached a status that saw to it that they remained intact. These entities were to oversee the distribution of lands to all enrolled members. As a further effort to erode tribal strength, there was the imposition of the blood quantum, to determine who, in government eyes, was Indian. This became an intregal part of the process undertaken by the Commission. The Commission determined that individuals had to be half or more of Indian blood to qualify. From a Traditionalist (culturally conservative) point of view, there were grounds for conflict. While some factions in tribal societies may have concurred, there were those who had felt other criteria had precedent as to what was good for the community. Things did not necessarily go smoothly with this process of transition. The Creeks were the last government to comply in 1901. There had been underlaying civil tensions in some of the relocated southeastern nations for decades. The circumstances that had started in the southeastern part of the continent again became prominent. The tribal governments in the eyes of the culturally conservative (Traditionalists), did not represent the true spirit of the culture. This was to lead to the Crazy Snake Uprisings of 1902 and 1907. Followers of Crazy Snake (Chitto Harjo) for the most part were full bloods and mixed bloods of African descent or those of African descent who had been lifelong residents of the Creek Nation. They steadfastly clung to the old ways and wanted no part of these events. Many had refused to take part in any facet of the enrollment process (this fact of nonenrollment, whether one can trace ancestry into Oklahoma or elsewhere, continues to be an issue in native circles throughout North America in particular). Chitto Harjo had been involved in the Green Peach War of 1882. This had also been an attempt to return to the more culturally conservative ways of Creek culture. In a show of patriotism, Dick Glass, who had gained infamy as an outlaw, led a group African- Creeks into battle during the hostilities. Mr. Glass, a member of the Creek Nation, was usually up to his endeavors in the areas covering the Creek and Cherokee Nations. He would be eventually run out of the Creek Nation, and move his activities to an area that ran from the Chickasaw Nation into the Choctaw Nation. Yet even though he was seen as an outlaw to some, to others, he was a respected member of a faction within the Creek Nation who tended to side with the Traditionalists. He would lose his life in a shootout with a posse who was led by the famed Cherokee lawman, Captain Sam Sixkiller of the U.S. Indian Police, in 1885. As it turned out, some units of the U.S. Army (cavalry) were involved in the federal intervention. The opposition representing the other point of view was the "Progressives", many of whom occupied positions in the tribal government. This faction took a more Assimilationist viewpoint. The United States Government had always found it politically convenient to deal with this faction, regardless of what nation. They (the federal government) had dealt with these factions in the earlier part of the 1800s, and, in doing so, established the premise that this was the faction that spoke for all of its people. The reality was quite different, as more culturally conservative elements within a respective nation saw and felt otherwise. Of course, when it came to oppression and policies that were to benefit the federal government as opposed to the native nations, the Assimilationists factions suffered the same as their more traditional brothers and sisters. There was an attempt to re-establish a more Traditionalist style-council system by the faction that was following Crazy Snake. This faction elected chiefs, a legislature, a court system and police force in the fall of 1900. When a letter was sent to President McKinley, that seemed to get the undivided attention of federal agencies. Things were to steamroll to the point where violence would erupt. Eventually, a contingent of U.S. Marshals and units of the Eighth Cavalry entered the Creek Nation to serve as the arm of federal intervention in the situation.

As the process of allotments proceeded, it was to become apparent that there were serious flaws in the way things were being handled. The dynamic of those that represented the Assimilationist viewpoint seemed to come out ahead. Those that were called traditionalist ended up at the bottom of the barrel. The racialist concepts that permeated mainstream American society was being felt stronger among the nations. For the African descendent residents of the Chickasaw Nation, there was to be a continuation of the struggle for citizenship. The other relocated southeastern nations had granted their African descent residents rights as citizens. The Seminole and Creek Nations had been the first to do so after the civil war. The Cherokees and Choctaws would do so later. The various incarnations (after the civil war) of the Chickasaw Government would not follow suit. Working on behalf of the Freedmen, the Chickasaw Freedmen's Association obtained the services of legal counsel. This was done clearly in the hope that several courses of action appealing to the tribal government as well as representatives of the federal government in the attempt would secure and guarantee what was best for their interest. The actions of the Dawes Commission further exacerbated an already awkward situation. There was a strange irony at work during this time. The struggle for citizenship in the Chickasaw Nation was an endeavor that the Freedmen had been striving for.

With the measures undertaken by the Dawes Commission, several phenomena took place. It is false to believe that the United States Government was acting in the interest of humanity and kindness. There was a specific motive being played out in this scenario. The federal government, perhaps alarmed of the prospect of having more people of African descent becoming citizens of the

United States, undertook measures to validate the Freedmen's claims to rights in the Chickasaw Nation. While this may initially seemed that this would benefit the Freedmen, the process of enrollment had serious flaws. There were ongoing efforts that had to constantly challenge the fact that any person of whatever degree of African blood was not entitled to the rights of citizenship, regardless of the fact that there was a quantum of Chickasaw blood. The Freedmen charged the Dawes Commission with violating the law by only recording their African descent and not their Chickasaw descent. By the records kept by the representatives of the federal government, there was no issue when the mix of ancestry was European and Chickasaw.

Similar to circumstances that existed in other parts of Oklahoma, while a governing body may have tried to exploit this situation, this attitude was not monolithic. There were factions of the citizenry that did not approve. The Freedmen, for sure, didn't. And those nation members who had relatives of African descent, in some cases spouses (African intermarriage was not approved of in the Chickasaw Nation) and certainly the children of these unions did not approve of the actions of the tribal governing body. The very fact that the federal government sought to intervene in the affairs of the Chickasaw Nation, showed the nation's sovereignty was being ignored. The Freedmen eventually obtained their allotments after a long legal battle. In the end, however, with the implementation of statehood for Oklahoma, the sovereignty of the native nations that had lived in that area ceased to exist, the self-sufficiency and autonomy undermined once again. And while the nations struggled and rebounded to some extent from this, another crisis created and imposed on them by an outside entity, the United States Government, things were never the same. At the time Oklahoma became a state, it officially became law that it was illegal for anyone not of African descent to marry anyone of African descent. Penalties for this phenomenon would include fines and imprisonment, when imposed. Given the fact that there was a scramble to exploit the oil and mineral resources that were present in the regions formerly identified as Indian Territory, this ruling would be utilized to the advantage of those who had the interest of white greed as an attitude. Specifically by defrauding those former residents of the territory, it was possible for the control of those resources to change hands. When it was politically convenient, courts would uphold this law as one that was to be applied retroactively, thus creating further barriers on the rights of those of African descent, whether they had native ancestry or not.

The beginning of the decline of the territory (in terms of further sovereignty infringement leading to the total loss of autonomy) started as business interests and the United States Government would begin to devise ways of legislating the Indian Territory out of the control of its inhabitants who, in many instances, were descended of people(s) forcefully relocated there during the time period of the 1830s, 40s, and 50s. Land hungry travelers would factor into this scenario as time and time again squatters would attempt to occupy lands in the territory that seemed "vacant". There were instances of U.S. Army units being ordered to escort these squatters out of the territory. But as time went on, these groups and individuals were to become increasingly vocal in wanting a piece of the action. To compound this, white residents of the different nations were becoming active in trying to gain more political power in the region. Initially, these residents, if not married to a member of a nation, had no say in the affairs of that particular nation. These are some of the factors that spelled the inevitable downfall of the nations.

Displacement.

People of diasporas around the world are living testimony to this condition. No doubt, there have been some Americans of African descent who for years fell into the belief that anything African was to be viewed with destain. Centuries of social conditioning by the dominant culture had found its way to many, including those who had ancestry who was supposedly despised. Indeed, there has been an ongoing effort by some in African -American communities to combat the relentless showering of negative images. These assaults take on many forms, ranging from the inadequate and often ignorant information provided in educational settings (schools) to the constant bombardment of negative stereotypes perpetuated by factions of the popular media. To a large extent, the roots of these negative images can be traced back to the beginnings of the slave trade and the invasion of the western hemisphere. Perversely, those who sought to conquer and enslave justified attitudes by whatever means were available. With the justification of these attitudes came the horrors that were perpetuated against Native Americans as well as Africans throughout the hemisphere. A "savage" was something less than human and had no rights that had to be respected. While it was economically convenient, members of the indigenous population had no rights that any white man had to respect. The Papal Bull issued out of the Vatican in 1493 by Pope Alexander VI added weight and justification to the exploitation of the inhabitants of what is now known as the Caribbean, and Central, South and North Americas. Known as the "Inter Caetera", this document declared that Spain was justified in taking whatever course of action as far as exploiting the peoples and lands of the western hemisphere. If the lands contacted were not under the rule of a Christian monarch, the sovereignty of the original inhabitants was, at best, invalid. In England during 1493, a commission of Henry VII authorized John Cabot and his sons to take possession of any non - Christian lands "discovered" (the Cabot Charter). Subsequent English rulers would continue to give explorers free reign to subjugate any peoples who stood in the way of imperial expansion. In the eyes of the Vatican which, at the time, was the source of moral inspiration to some of the European countries vying to control the western hemisphere, as well as in courts of numerous European nations, the fact of prior occupation of the encountered territories was not an issue if the people there did not share the same spiritual belief system(s) and skin color. If the people of any area were not Christian, they were "heathen". Heathens were (and still are in the minds of some today) less than human, thus entitled to nothing except what could be done to them. The enslavement of the people, and the theft of territory, were all up for grabs by the Spanish, Portuguese, English, French, and the Dutch.

The presumption was that anything Christian, especially with European trappings, was the superior culture (not taking into account the often bloody rivalries between the nations of Europe). In the realm of the expansion implemented by Spain, the intervention of the Christian priest Bartoleme De Las Casas would deter (somewhat) the horrific onslaught that was in the beginning stages of victimizing the populations of the hemisphere (although Las Casas found humanity in the peoples of the Caribbean. Africans were another matter altogether). This was happening in spite of the fact(s) that cultures on both sides of the Atlantic were (are) richly complex in their cultural retention and expressions and, in many instances had made many contributions to the world theater. The bottom line was that there was land to be seized and bodies to be taken.

It is still the exception rather than the rule that when there is the mention of things African and/or Native American, there are usually images that arise, and these images do not reflect the entire picture. And this is if the images portrayed reflect any kind of accuracy to begin with. The picture painted is to begin in line with the concept of "flavor of the month", and this is usually only paying lip service to whatever culture is chic at that moment. The exploitation of aspects of Native American and African cultures continues under different guises. Rarely are places like Cahokia mentioned, which was one of the largest urban centers in North America prior to the invasion of 1492. This city, which was at its peak around AD 1100, was a trade center that drew travelers from regions all over the hemisphere by land and water routes. The general public knows the area where Cahokia once stood now as St. Louis. Further north on the Mississippi River, where Rock Island is now located in the area that would eventually be known as part of the state of Illinois, the city of Saukenuk would rise. Located on more than three thousand acres, this urban settlement was the home to more than eleven thousand people of the Sac and Fox Union. The city itself was neatly arranged in blocks, and it would astonish early Europeans who traveled in the region. Tenotchitlan has been addressed to some extent, but not extensively (at least not in the United States). In-depth discussions seem to be limited to academic and specific cultural circles. This great city was "grander than anything in Europe" stated a member of Cortez's entourage in the 1520s. This area is known today as Mexico City. Outside of cultural and some academic circles are the scientific, medicinal, culinary, and other contributions by Native Americans not mentioned at length. Similarly, it is rare that the great cities of Africa mentioned, such as Timbukto, Djenne, or Zimbabwe. Positive contributions to the world are still rarely spoken of outside of some academic and Afrocentric circles. If these facts are brought to light for the general public, there always seems to be a source that claims their existence and origins have their roots somewhere in Europe. These kinds of attitudes and the perpetuation of imagery that stems from them feeds into mindsets that are damaging to those of the ancestry of the Americas,

Africa, and/or any combination thereof. It is certainly arguable that humanity as a whole suffers when the contributions of any people are denied.

Some of the roots of the perpetuation of stereotypes can be traced back to the events growing out of the landing of Christopher Columbus and crew on the island of Guanahani on October 12, 1492. It would not be advantageous to depict cultures contacted as having any merit on their own. While images of most indigenous and African cultures in the minds of dominant society tend to view rural peoples as the norm, this certainly was not the entire picture. On both sides of the Atlantic Ocean, there were urban societies that had, in their midst, learning centers. Libraries in Africa and the western hemisphere fell under the torches of the conquerors. The more ignorant and supposedly backward a people were (are), the easier it was (is) to take away what is rightfully theirs. If the spiritual beliefs of a people or peoples are deemed at best superficial (if they are acknowledged at all), then these people(s) need their souls saved. In the minds of those who were using Christianity as a weapon against the cultures encountered, the use of traditional items such as drums, dancing, etc., further reinforced that these people were, in fact, "heathens" and "savages". The entertainment industry continues to play on old apprehensions by portraying any dark- skinned peoples engaging in the pursuit and practice of their respective belief systems (especially where drums are used) as something evil and degrading. The sensationalizing of Vodum, Candomble, Macumba, Obeah, Santeria, the Sun Dance, the Ghost Dance, Potlatch, etc., translates (in contemporary times) to box office sales. Cultural context and accuracy is not a priority, much less a consideration. What happens to the bodies, territory, and culture at the hands of the conqueror is what "they" deserve to have happen. And if their bodies and souls could not be taken, their lives would be. Historically, those who opposed and attempted to defend their communities further gave fuel to other notions of negativity. During the time Europeans tried to conquer them, the Caribs were said to practice cannibalism. To this day, it has never been proven that the Caribs engaged in this practice. Yet these stories made it easier to demonize these people of the Antilles. The English would use these stories in the attempt to scare enslaved Africans from running away to the Caribs. If anything, the Caribs were guilty of fighting fiercely to protect what was theirs and doing so for a substantial length of time. The reality of the hemispheric invasion was the victims had little to say as far as anything was concerned that would make a difference in the attitudes of the invaders.

Ironically, the descendants of the original victims often fall for the negative stereotypes. If your culture is constantly portrayed as less than dignified or, in the extreme, portrayed and reinforced as being extinct, there has been a tendency by some to distance themselves from something that appears to be good for nothing but ridicule and worse. With the rise and popularity of moving pictures, films have played a major role in reinforcing negativity. During the mid twentieth century, millions of people watched regularly as Tarzan singlehandedly outwitted and killed scores of "Natives", then always make his escape into the jungle where there was a network of vines that make the New York City subway system look like a one-lane country road. A handful of white cowboys and/or backwoodsmen were constantly seen killing Native Americans by the hundreds in the majority of frontier/western action films coming out of Hollywood, California in this era. The irony here was that initially, there were white "cowhands". The title of "Cowboy" was first used to designate those men of African descent, native descent, or any combination of both. For many people, the images where people of color were constantly being defeated in Africa and the American west were the only images available of indigenous people and Africans for a long time.

To a certain extent, those Native Americans who reside in geographic concentrations are fortunate. This is not to trivialize and downplay the conditions on many reservations. Situations like the Mashantucket Pequots of Connecticut, the Seminole Tribe of Florida, The Passamaquoddy of Maine, or the Choctaws of Mississippi (some nations that have realized economic success through their efforts) are not the norm for many reservation communities. While there continues to be economic endeavors undertaken in many communities such as cattle ranching, communications (radio), tourism, and manufacturing (among other activities), some reservation communities have been called, usually by outsiders, rural ghettos or projects. This type of terminology has been deemed offensive by some of the residents of those communities. There remains the fact that poverty is no stranger in many of these areas. Poverty is rampant in many communities, and along with this comes the myriad of problems that characterize this condition. High unemployment is often the rule, not the exception. During the winter of 1996-97, eight people froze to death on several reservations in the Dakotas due to inadequate housing. During the summer of 2001, some residents of native communities in northern California were asked how they managed in times of the increasing frequent power outages. Many of the people there responded that it made no difference because many of these communities had no electric power to begin with. Similar situations continue to plague urban settings as well. Yet in spite of what can seem to be overwhelming hardships, on the reservation, people are in close proximity to each other. After decades of oppressive measures aimed at these communities, some have begun to reassert themselves culturally. This reinforces a sense of identity, although this sense of identity often remains under attack by forces from outside the community. In the eyes of the community, as well as to the outside world, the representation of things that are "real Indian" exists. What about those who are descended from ancestral sources who experienced the misfortune of being separated from what was culturally familiar? What are the circumstances that has led to this? Voluntary relocation? Forced relocation? How has the passage of time widened the gap between those who share similar roots but are now distant?

The history of Africa and the numerous nations of Turtle Island is tragically full of examples that illustrate the effects of separation from one's culture. The victims of slavers on both sides of the Atlantic Ocean found themselves thrown into a situation that, at the least, sought to destroy all that defined the sense of humanity rising from specific cultural perspectives. Even though in some instances the enslavers sought to save the souls of their victims, the value system forced on the enslaved continued to be demeaning. What was done under the guises and in the name(s) of monotheistic religions played into the system that maintained the status quo of the times by justifying the necessary enslavement of dark peoples, be they African, Native American, Asian, or any combination thereof. In the western hemisphere those who found themselves in the slave quarters of the Caribbean or, North, South, Central America, were thrust into a world that relentlessly attempted to destroy all they possessed. By this point in time, this included (but was not restricted to) the sense of dignity. Here, all the enslaved people were good for was the will of the slavemaster, and in turn, they play into the scheme of having societies built through their sweat, blood, and anguish. For those who had originated in Africa, they were no longer to be known as Mensa, Kwesi, Obatunde, Byabinge, or Fanta. No longer were they to be known as Bambara, Fon, Ibo, Ewe, Yoruba, or Hausa. As the spirit of resistance became dominant, those who found themselves in the situation of maroon settlements realized that under the circumstances, they would have to become one nation. This was happening because the residents of these societies were Ibo, Wolof, Fon, Dahomey, and so on. Various African cultures started to merge with each other out of the real necessity of survival. Depending on where this was occurring, more than likely, elements of Native American cultures made themselves known. One can look at Brazil, Mexico, Suriname, and regions in what is now called the United States, such as Louisiana, just as some examples. For those with origins in the western hemisphere, the fact that one was Wampanoag, Nipmuc, Tuscarora, Canarsee, Reckawawank, Cherokee, Oconee, Wacamaw, Pedee, Houma, Caddo, Pawnee, etc., was irrelevant. Slaves, in the eyes of the authorities of the time, were less than human, thus, they had no right(s) to any sense of dignity and/or identity unless the sense of identity was forced on them by the slaveholding class. These attitudes filtered out into the mainstream population. Yet as different European countries gained control of the regions in the western hemisphere, the phenomenon of shifting alliances became prevalent. Again, this was happening as a result of the need to survive under the immediate circumstance of crises. As countries such as France and England jockeyed for territorial advantages throughout what is now the eastern United States, some indigenous nations that had been traditional enemies found they needed each other if they were to survive. With the onset of the War of Independence, nations that had formerly been cohesive became fragmented to the point of civil war. In some cases, like the Cherokees, the seeds of change and mistrust were planted, and this factionalism would grow to cause outbreaks of violence that traced their causes back to the mid 1700s. New communities came together as a result of the changes brought on directly or indirectly by the actions of different European countries. What was known as the Creek Confederacy covering areas of Alabama and Georgia constantly absorbed groups that were the victims of turmoil. The Catawbas of South Carolina took in peoples of smaller nations who had been threatened by destruction. Fort Niagara, located on the southwestern shore of Lake Ontario, was one of several English strongholds that launched expeditions at the then upstart of American colonies. The area surrounding the fort and for miles around became the location of a massive refugee settlement as peoples such as the Mahican, Narragansett, Saponi, Montauks, Wappingers, Nanticokes, Shawnee, and Tuscarora (to name a few) sought to rebuild their lives in the midst of war. Many of the camps near the fort were already the locations of the villages of the Haudenosaunee (Iroquois Confederacy). Where as many of these refugees had been enemies of the Iroquois, they were now welcome, and new multicultural societies began to emerge. Although traits of a specific culture may have dominated, other cultures being in close proximity to each other were bound to influence one another.

In many parts of North America, the singing of traditional songs, the possession and use of drums, the speaking of native languages, and almost any kind of cultural retention was outlawed. Attempts at maintaining one's culture had to be conducted under the most extreme conditions of secrecy, for discovery would lead to punishment of varying degrees and intensity. One of these examples was when native children were forced into boarding schools, and they were physically abused for speaking their own language. As many different types of people found themselves in close proximity because of the circumstance of slavery, Ewe met Muscogee, Tuscarora met Yoruba, Taino met Wolof, etc., mutual acculturation began, whether one wanted it to happen or not. With the intensification of slave raids that led into the very hearts of settlements in any given area, chaos and terror was the order of the day. It will probably never be known specifically how many people perished in the vast lands on both sides of the Atlantic Ocean by attempting to escape raids that caught them by surprise. In some instances, the escapees had to be wary of pursuit. Even if the pursuers were avoided, untold numbers of people more than likely met a tragic fate deep in the forests or swamps, succumbing to animal attacks or any other surprises the environment yielded, such as quicksand. There are stories handed down in the culture of the Florida Seminoles that tell of frantic mothers having to leave their babies in holes in the ground, covered by leaves in the hopes of being able to return at a later time to retrieve their young ones. There were also rumors of infanticide, which was done when it was apparent that the cries of infants could attract the attention of any number of enemies who were seeking out the groups that had fled in the face of relentless efforts.

In some instances, individuals made their way into either white or black societies. It was dangerous to visibly maintain one's birth culture in these circumstances, as the authorities of the time could react in any manner of ways, none of which had the welfare and wellbeing of persons in mind. Thus, a man or woman would secretly tell their descendants, be they children and/or grandchildren that they were Lenape, Creek, Cherokee, Saponi, Yamasee, Siwanoy, Taino, etc. Or perhaps the elder would tell their descendants prayers to the Orishas, chants in Akan, or pray to the east as often as possible during the day. The grandmother or grandfather might have secretly taught words like Wah-Nee, Ishtay, Osiyo, Ahleecoobah, Tao- tee, Alafia, En-Yah Tah-Fey, or Habari Gani. Songs and/or rituals were told either in part or entirely. This elder may have been in demand in rural areas because of his or her knowledge of healing plants. As generation after generation passed, the origins of this knowledge in some cases may not have been acknowledged, or forgotten altogether. Yet at family gatherings or other familiar settings stories or possibly quick statements may have been mentioned in passing "Your Grandmother/father was Apalachee, Creek, Cherokee, etc. During the twentieth century there were waves of migrations into urban areas. In some cases, it would be individuals or sometimes families leaving reservations in the hopes of finding better opportunities. In other instances, families and individuals migrated to urban areas after being led to believe that there would be support systems that would enable them to survive until they were established (decent job, housing etc.). In other cases, there were to be successive waves of migrations from the rural south from African-American communities. With these occurrences, other dynamics would come into play. Established urban dwellers frowned down on anything "country". For those that had (knowingly or un-knowingly) bought into stereotypic images, only city things were cool, thus socially acceptable. Anything outside of these standard was not acceptable. For the person(s) who had migrated from the countryside of Georgia, Alabama, North or South Carolina, Florida or Virginia (to name a few) they were now in the midst of an urban setting. The stories that were once respected, even in secrecy, were no longer worthy of respect. The elder may had found him or herself the recipient of patient or not so patient attitudes from family members who had let another set of priorities supersede the passing down of oral history, something that had possibly survived centuries. As a result, the descendants of those who had suffered because of negative endeavors (i.e., war, slavery, land theft), that had been waged against their ancestors unwittingly played into the scheme of cultural genocide.

It is significant to look at the periods of rural to urban movement. Sometimes individuals or families left reservations to seek opportunities in major cities. In these settings, people were often confronted with a range of situations that were antagonistic. Racists stereotypes create scenarios that are at the least, detrimental. This is a reality that people of color have consistently had to find ways of dealing with. In spite of this, people have found ways of surviving. Urban America certainly can thank the Skywalkers for their skill in helping construct many of the large skyscrapers of some of North America's cities. Mohawk, as well as other Iroquois men, have continuously filled the ranks of high steel workers for decades (as fate would have it, there was a construction crew of Mohawk men working on a building near the World Trade Center on 9/11/2001. Some of their relatives had worked on the construction of the two towers decades earlier). Eventually, native community centers would be established to assist people who felt alienation in the urban setting and deal with environments that were at times hostile to their presence. There were other stories that migrated to urban areas. There were those whose families had kept alive the history of their ancestry in varying degrees. The 1940s, 50s, and 60s saw large migrations of African-Americans out of the south, to large urban centers, primarily in the north. Those of African-Native descent who were not from reservation communities, or settings where there would be large concentrations of people in close proximity to each other, nonetheless brought with themselves this history to urban settings as well. There were varying degrees of disdain from those who had a history of residing in an urban setting for anything "country". In many instances, the new migrants from any number of rural settings certainly lived up to the expectations of these city folks. Because of these types of prevailing attitudes, combined with the results of centuries of divide and conquer tactics that shaped sociopolitical attitudes, many of the retention of heritage were often suppressed or outrightly dismissed as the transplanted southerners tried to adopt and assimilate into a more (supposedly) sophisticated lifestyle(s).

Not all movement was done by a respective community as a whole. Some individuals left the community because of a variety of reasons. The time period and circumstances that would lead an individual into other social situations were as varied as the stars in the sky. Sometimes it was because there was no longer a community with which to stay. Slave raids, disease, and military actions (which often went hand in hand with slave raids) obliterated smaller nations. Individuals under these circumstances found their way to situations that led to the beginnings of other societies, or strengthened existing ones by adding to the population numbers. Just as there were those who married into other native communities, some married out and found their way to white or black communities. If a person had a skill or set of skills to offer, this could lead to other options, even in the face of obstacles created by racism. Farming, manual labor, carpentry, and blacksmithing, were some skills that, in turn, led to options. There were other situations. During the time of colonization of the hemisphere, the demand for hides and pelts of different animals led some men far from white settlements (both frontier and mainstream). This meant transiting and living in areas that placed them in contact with various native cultures. As a means of survival, many of these men who could be described as "rugged individualists", adapted skills from native cultures and learned means of communicating with various nations. Such was the case in North America, where a person could strike out and carve a place for himself in the expanses beyond white society at that time. For someone escaping slavery, taking chances with indigenous societies and whatever the natural environment provided was seen as a better option. At least one was free, as long as white society remained distant. The results of people interacting and influencing each other lead to new endeavors. In the late 1700s a man by the name of Jean Baptiste DuSable traveled northward. It was said that he was an escaped slave, possibly from Haiti. Establishing himself in an area, he was to marry a Potawatomi woman known as Catherine, and the location of his home was Eschikagou, an Algonquin term, meaning "Place of Wild Onions". Today, this area is called Chicago. While DuSable and his family lived in the area, he had interactions with many different people of all backgrounds. The Bonga family was to be known for generations in Minnesota establishing roots in the area now called Duluth. It is said that the elders of this legacy were slaves brought into Minnesota from Canada sometime during the late 1700s. The son of this couple, Pierre Bonga, became an interpreter, interacting with the Chippewa people. Pierre Bonga married a Chippewa woman, and this couple established themselves in the area today called Duluth. Their son, George, would establish himself as a trapper and trader who was well respected. George Bonga learned the ways of many, being schooled in Montreal as well as among his mother's people. He spoke Chippewa, French, and English, and was known to be fluent in other native languages. Among his many accomplishments was that of assisting Governor Lewis Cass of Minnesota with the Treaty of 1837. The Bonga Family legacy is still evident in Cass County, Minnesota. Bonga Township is the testimony to those of the family who settled in the area.

The United States Government's plans for Native Americans did not always manifest itself in military actions. After the subjugation of some of the original inhabitants, it was determined that the best course of action was to bring native peoples into white culture. The irony of this was that racism would continue to at best marginalize anyone who wasn't white. In the minds of some, native peoples would be better off taking on the trappings of white America. One policy was the placing of native children into white households. This lasted well into the 20th century. Another policy was that of taking children and sending them to schools often hundreds, if not thousands of miles away from their communities. This was detrimental on many levels. The scenarios the children and young people faced extended horrifically beyond culture shock. Those young boys who were from cultures that held long hair in esteem were forced to have their hair cut. Children were subject to corporal punishment if they spoke their native languages. Some children who found it hard to adapt to these new circumstances attempted to run away. Others attempted and sometimes committed suicide. For those who were able to adapt and, after a time, were returned to the communities of their origins, they would at times encounter marginalization, as some communities (themselves undergoing social transformation, which may not have necessarily been a smooth transition) found their children changed into something that was not socially/culturally acceptable. Some of these schools such as the Carlise School in Pennsylvania were to be occupied exclusively by native children. Yet there was another situation happening in Virginia. The Hampton Institute was a school for African Americans of both genders. By the late 1800's the U.S. Government began initially placing young men from Plains culture(s) in the school. As time went on, the new arrivals began to reflect the phenomenon of young people from increasingly diverse backgrounds who were to attend the school. As more young people from relocated eastern nations began to appear, it was clear that some were of multiple ancestry. While this had occurred to varying degrees with some of the Plains people who had arrived earlier at the institution, as the dynamic shifted it was apparent that the legacy of racial interaction characterized within cultures from the east and southeast, in particular, was evident.

The longing and/or journey back to geographic communities (be they reservation, territory, or country) itself yielded its own set of obstacles. The Trans-Atlantic Slave Trade by and large made specific identification of African peoples monumental at best. Once Africans arrived in the western hemisphere (after 1492), other factors further complicated matters if one was to consider trying to trace specific African roots. Africans from different nations and ethnic groups were brought together, especially when these kidnapped victims were taken into

North America. Men and women of different ethnic backgrounds intermarried, often because there was little choice. Ewe met Yoruba, Ibo met Dahomey, Bambara met Wolof, etc. Women of color, be they African or indigenous, or any combination thereof were considered open prey in the eyes of some white men, and as a result these women became victims of sexual abuse. There was also the factor of love, which certainly crossed racial and ethnic lines. Indigenous people and Africans intermarried, as well as in other instances where Europeans figured in the mix. A former colleague (of mine) who had been a Peace Corps volunteer once stated that what was considered a "mixed" marriage in (sub- Saharan) Africa would never be considered so in any part of the western hemisphere. She had witnessed a wedding of two people from two different ethnic groups in Sierra Leone, which had caused consternation among people in the particular area. As triumphant as it was, situations like that of the late writer Alex Haley tracing his heritage back to a specific village in West Africa, are still sadly (largely) the exception, not the rule. Africans in the western hemisphere (after 1492) of varying ethnic groups came together out of necessity. Similarly, some Native Americans (such as the Shawnee patriot Tecumseh) realized that in the face of ongoing dislocations caused by any number of factors surrounding European expansion throughout the Caribbean, North, South, and Central America, that it was in the best interest of all parties concerned to come together. While an individual may have the bloodlines to a specific group of people, tracing the lines definitively had (has) its difficulties when approaching a community that, for any number of reasons, looks upon "outsiders" with skepticism. Further complicating this is where the knowledge of Clan affiliation has been lost (among south eastern people, for example, the Clan is of importance). In some instances, the Clan may have died out with the last of a bloodline or relocated hundreds of miles elsewhere, such as in the case of forced migrations out of the southeast into Oklahoma. The imposition of blood quantum qualification also impacts on the search to identify lost family. In some instances where individuals were met with barriers that appear(ed) insurmountable when contacting a community (for example), the search for cultural support out of necessity took on a different quest. It is interesting that in the decades of the mid and late twentieth century the proliferation of community-based organizations in urban, as well as some rural, areas became evident. Some of these groups were (are) nation-specific (i.e. Cherokee). This in of itself is not a unique situation. In states like Virginia, and South Carolina, as well as other mid-atlantic states, numerous civic groups were formed to deal specifically with indigenous issues. Some of these organizations clearly identified with specific cultures where there were roots, such as the Pee Dee Indian Association (South Carolina), and the United Rappahannock (Virginia). The focus here is that these groups that were formed represented people who were still in close proximity to their traditional homelands. In other areas, support groups that were formed often were (are) comprised of a membership that had been dislocated from their homelands, for whatever reason. Some of these groups are comprised of individuals from many nations, thus, their organization is intertribal in nature. It can be speculated that in a different time period (the past), these types of community organizations would have formed geographic communities of their own. This would have been depended on a land base. In light of the onslaught to take away lands from Native Americans, any areas used as a base for a community would have been, out of necessity isolated, and of no use or interest to the expansionistic goals of European countries of that era. This has been the norm as people struggle to maintain control over their lives in the face of adversity. Many multicultural (intertribal) communities arose out of situations like this to be eventually specified under one identity. What seems to be the common ground with many of these groups is they provide varying degrees of support, and a unifying presence to some peoples who represent those who have been dislocated. This is necessary, as the pressures of the dominant culture have continued attempts to define, dominate, and dictate what the sense of identity is. And this has happened in an atmosphere that continues to have conflicts from within, as numerous peoples deal with, on an ongoing basis, what it means to be native, the issues of sovereignty, who their relations are, and (as happens throughout the United States) who is eligible for tribal enrollment. But these issues are certainly not restricted to any one group of people. In April of 1997, sects of Orthodox Jews in the United States and Israel attempted to define who is a Jew and who is not, setting into motion controversy in Jewish communities throughout the world. In some cultures, there is an underlying (and sometimes not so underlying) air in some circles of the ongoing obsession with skin color variation (light-skinned and dark-skinned). During and, to a certain extent, after the (mass) resurgence of black pride in the United States during the 1960s, it was not uncommon to hear, in some circles in African-American communities accusations of who is more black than whoever or whatever. Some individuals who migrated to the United States from places like Cuba, Puerto Rico, Brazil, grew up in an atmosphere that was Afrocentric. As a result, many people from these regions (as well as from other areas of the Caribbean, and Central, and South America) consider themselves African, regardless of their skin color. Yet (especially in the 70s, 80s and early 90s), when meeting some African-Americans, they were puzzled that some of the children of the African Diaspora born and raised in the United States had little idea of the African retention that was (is) common in other parts of the western hemisphere. In settings of cultural privacy in some parts of Native America, many deal with the issue of who is Indian and who is not. This continues in the face of hundreds of years of intermarriage with Africans, Europeans, and Asians. The phenomenon of multiple ancestry has been used on an ongoing basis by some interests within government agencies, and some instances the private sector, that sees it to their advantage to dictate who is what (racially/ethnically speaking). In some areas of the south and mid-atlantic states, there exist communities that are multiracial in character and for all- extensive purposes, have been marginalized from mainstream America. Terms such as Melungeon, Redbone, and Tri-Racial Isolates have been used to describe these communities. The origin of this terminology did not emerge from within these communities. The terms were (are) used by outsiders attempting to characterize residents of these communities. In 1997, when champion golf pro Tiger Woods stated that he is proud of all of his ancestry (Native American, African, and Asian), some in African- American communities were quick to respond how he was denying his blackness. Acknowledging and not just playing lip service to one's ancestry, especially multiple ancestry, is still a flashpoint and can spark controversy in some circles. Thus, where there had existed systems within a given culture (such as some indigenous cultures of the United States) that had successfully acculturated others into their respective societies, the constant intervention of outside forces created atmospheres that are, in the least, disruptive. This is the price of attempting to conduct oneself with dignity in a highly racialized environment. The gap and divisions that have resulted as a product of divide and conquer tactics further isolates African-American and indigenous communities from each other, regardless of the fact that there are often shared bloodlines. During the United States period of Apartheid, known as Segregation, some indigenous communities were under constant pressure to be legislated out of whatever remaining resources were at hand (i.e. land). If a community was proven to be "negro" or "colored", the respective community found themselves legislated into a sociopolitical status that was down another notch on the detriment scale. Since African-Americans, and Native Americans were the victims of the same Jim Crow Laws, to be legally classified as "colored" opened the door for whatever remaining land base a respective community had and/or resources to be taken away. It was advantageous for the dominant culture to view the multiracial status of some communities as a means to an end, and anything not fitting neatly into politically convenient racial/ethnic categories was a wild card that was to be eliminated. It became seemingly in the best interest of some indigenous communities to put as much distance between themselves and African-American communities.

Ironically, through legislation, government entities by placing African-Americans and Native Americans in the same legal category, it has reversed earlier attempts to separate the groups, which in some instances had become one in the same because of intermarriage and acculturation. The effects of these actions left scars on the psyche of many of these communities. And where there was intermarriage within a given community, the results were devastating as families found themselves responding to crises created by outside forces. Some felt there was a choice to be made and decided to acknowledge one part of ancestry over the other. These types of efforts have undermined potential alliances and partnerships that could be beneficial for those who continue to be victimized by these sorts of attacks. In the twenty first century, these kinds of scenarios are still real.

Even in the twenty first century, where some communities of color seem to make strides on the road to economic sufficiency and autonomy, the backlash syndrome rears its head again and again. This is no stranger to African-American business people who begin to realize some degree of success from their endeavors, and Native American business endeavors just as often come between the crosshairs of what can be labeled as overzealous scrutiny. Where some nations have made strides through various economic endeavors such as those undertaken by the Mississippi Band of Choctaw Indians, the Passamoquoddy of Maine, the Seminole Tribe of Florida, and the Mashantucket Pequot Nation (for example), government and or big-business interests (but not isolated to these groups) have a habit of taking scrutiny to some additional horizons. A parallel that seems to affect the Seminole Tribe of Florida and the Mashantucket Peqout Nation of Connecticut (among other things) is a backlash aimed at these sovereign entities that have undertaken to obtain lands that were originally part of their legacy of custodianship. These lands were the same areas that were taken from these nations by strategies and actions that are best characterized as genocidal. A more accurate way to characterize this kind of scrutiny is perversion. When endeavors are successful by entrepenuers in urban settings, especially when those involved parties are of color, similar tactics of scrutiny also apply. During the 1990s and the beginning years of the 2000s, it is the gains of people of color that are constantly attacked. In this atmosphere reversals at the legislative level, policies at the judicial level, which see disproportionate numbers of people of color imprisoned, increases of police misconduct in communities of color, and overall violence against people of color have become commonplace. Yet this is unfortunately nothing new. There are various points in the history of the United States where this was the norm and. at times, there was the influence of government officials who fed the atmosphere that led to this type of disposition in the minds of those who felt they had sanction to wreak havoc in whatever way, shape, or form on anyone or anybody that was (is) under the influence of melanin.

Some communities which, at times, have been characterized by outsiders as ghettoes in the wilderness, suffer from the same syndromes as their urban counterparts, where environmental racism rears its head (poor communities, regardless of color, tend to fall in this category). As some urban areas see abnormally high rates of asthma a (common denominator here is that there always seems to be high volumes of garbage-burning facilities and diesel-powered vehicles transiting these areas), rural areas reel from the effects of toxic waste contamination. In some instances, those wastes are nuclear. In other instances, corporations exploit the resources of an area and/or alter the land itself by flooding large tracks of territory. This happened in areas inhabited by Cree people who lived by subsistence hunting in Quebec, Canada, during dam construction in the latter part of the twentieth century. Toxic waste dumped in water sources like those in aquatic channels in the Great Lakes region, where Mohawk communities of New York and Canada bear the brunt of the dangers, mining as what had happened in the territory of the Lakotas during the 1970s, or in areas of the southwest where many Hopi and Dine (Navajo) lived, suffered as a result of environmental pollution. The area that has for centuries been held sacred by the Dine and Hopi peoples was designated as a "National Sacrifice Area". This covers what is known as the Four Corners, where New Mexico, Arizona, Colorado, and Utah meet. Southwestern native communities certainly did not fall victim to this type of activity only in the 1970s. During the era of early nuclear testing, specifically the testing of the devices that would lead to the first atomic bombs in the 1940s, some native communities were within wind range of nuclear fallout that was a result of the tests. Cancer rates skyrocketed in these communities in the period of time following the explosion of the device. The situation at Pine Ridge Reservation of the Lakota exploded into violence during the early 1970s as factions within the community reacted in a climate that had reached the breaking point. Against this backdrop was the fact that more than a dozen corporations were exploiting the natural resources of the reservation, and polluting the environment in the process. Some of these corporations were also active in Dine Territory. The roots of the issues affecting the Lakota can be traced back to the initial (white) incursion onto the Black Hills during the 1860s and 70s. At this point in time (the 1970s), it wasn't gold that triggered the lust to exploit. Uranium deposits were discovered, and this spelled dollars to big business. The actions undertaken by these corporations had the support of some federal agencies. The endeavors undertaken in this instance were in violation of the Fort Laramie Treaty of 1868, although this was hardly a unique situation nor precedent. This region is held in high spiritual esteem by the Lakota people. At the height of the confrontation in 1973, members of the American Indian Movement (A.I.M.) and some traditional Lakotas faced off against not only a police force from the reservation that followed the orders of an individual (Dick Wilson) that seemed to stop at nothing to administer his way, but, also the F.B.I., units of the South Dakota State Police, the U.S. Marshals, and units of the U.S. Army and U.S. Air Force. Dozens of deaths occurred to many standing up for the rights of their people, and in 2004 (when this book was completed), A.I.M. member Leonard Peltier is still a political prisoner. Violence from outsiders was nothing new to this region, as this confrontation at Wounded Knee was the second encounter of this kind. Its precedent on December 29, 1890, when two hundred sixty Hunkpapa men, women and children were shot by members of the Seventh Cavalry of the U.S. Army (this was George A. Custers' unit). This was happening in an atmosphere brought on by fear, as a religious movement was sweeping many native communities throughout the West. Prior to the events at Wounded Knee (1973), the Black Panther Party had been decimated after years of infiltration by agent provocateurs and armed assaults by various police agencies around the United States. What was common suspicion to those involved in the anti-war and civil rights struggles of the late 1960s and early 1970s was that the federal government was somehow behind these actions. As time passed, it became clear that a covert government operation known as Cointelpro was responsible for what had happened to many groups and organizations that were dissident voices.

Some areas of southwestern reservations (such as Dine) bear witness to high instances of radiation poisoning, along with its residual effects. Runoff from sugar crops in Florida had a direct effect on Seminole and Miccosukee communities in Southern Florida as areas of the Everglades down to portions of the southern tip of the peninsula were heavily impacted (during the mid and late twentieth century). Communities on the island of Vieques near Borinken (more commonly called Puerto Rico) that had lived in the shadow of a former U.S. Navy bombing range witness high degrees of cancer. And this is not taking into account that the livelihood of many residents of this island has been severely disrupted as military activities interfered with fishing patterns that had been utilized in better days. These are only a few examples. Some native communities still do not have the basics for a decent standard of living. The community of Shinnecock in Southampton, New York, experienced high degrees of cancer among their nation, which was traced to the use of their water supply. Having no wells, the community relied on a water source that has been contaminated by pesticide runoffs from farms that were once prevalent near their reservation. These acts were (are) carried out without any regard for the inhabits of the land, beyond token gestures. In the wake of these actions, water sources are often contaminated, threatening a vital community resource. Soil becomes depleted, leading to losses in farming opportunities and/or destroying habitats for native plant and animal species. In some of these cases, indigenous communities have lived in balance with these species in their respective areas for hundreds, if not thousands, of years. Parallels are noticed when examining communities of color in urban and rural settings in that there seems to be high degrees of illnesses that can be traced to environmental factors. In parts of New York City, neighborhoods with high asthma rates tend to be locales where there are high instances of diesel traffic transiting these areas on a regular basis. In recent times, these communities have mobilized to stop efforts to locate waste disposal facilities in their midst. Environmental and human exploitation is certainly not restricted to North America. Similar situations can be examined in Central and South America, and islands and their surrounding habitats of the Pacific Ocean, Africa, etc. These are sadly only a few examples that indicate environmental racism is a functioning reality.

A Cowboy of African descent made a find in New Mexico during the mid 1920s. This man, George McJunkin, set into motion a wave that hit the archeological establishment. Searching for lost cattle one day he came upon some bones, in which he found an arrowhead unlike any other he had seen. The bones and the arrowhead were to find their way into scientific circles. It seems that Mr. McJunkin had come upon what was left of a hunting party that was active during the time of the Ice Age. The Lakota Sioux Dance Theater touring West Africa in the early 1990s. In New York City, the Forces of Nature Dance Company, and the Thunderbird American Indian Dancers collaborated artistically during the 1990's. On her website, Martha Redbone, the 2002 Native American Music Awards Debut Artist of the Year humbly acknowledged the blessing of being "a link in the bridge" between the Native American and African-American communities. These are only some of the commonalities experienced. On the negative side, corporate and/or military exploitation of natural and human resources in the Americas, be it the Amazon, South Dakota, Columbia, the New York- Canada border, northeast Canada, Hawaii, Puerto Rico, New Mexico, or areas of Africa, such as Nigeria or (at one time) South Africa, the brutal repression of the Black Panther Party and the American Indian Movement in the 1960s and 70s (along with other groups that stood up in the face of social abuses) also are a testimony in the commonality of experiences. The denial of nation-to-nation status where the question of ethnic purity is perversely examined to be used against a specific group of people (i.e.tribe), stands in testimony of some indignities endured. In the United States this has happened time and time again where a question of who is "Indian" is dictated to communities of people (to varying degrees) at the mercy of the whims of outside entities. Indeed, it was not unusual during the era of overt discrimination that the same laws used to oppress people of African descent were also aimed at native populations. North Carolina's "Free Negro Code" of 1836 is only one example. The topic of blood quantum has been an issue bordering on explosive in communities of the United States, as well as in segments of the mainstream population. Indeed, during the late 1880s and 1890s when the Dawes Act was being implemented, part of the criteria for qualifying in the eyes of the United States Government and those who looked out for their interest was that one had to be of 1/2 or more Indian blood, not a member of a respective nation. What was accomplished by military means at other points in time was (is) approached increasingly by other tactics. In some instances, judicial and/or legislative actions have rendered, at least in the eyes of mainstream society, numerous communities of peoples to be extinct when it was (is) politically convenient to do so. On paper, it is possible in the eyes of government to legislate people out of existence. The Tainos of the Caribbean were the first in the western hemisphere to experience this type of designation and indignity. The Spanish, as well as other European invaders in the region, declared the Tainos extinct on island after island throughout the Caribbean time and time again. As in other instances when government entities look for rationales that served their needs, part of the reasoning the Tainos were "extinct" was because of intermarriage. The excuse of racial purity is a theme that has continued to be implemented wherever convenient. In earlier times, specifically during the era after the initial invasion of 1492, colonial authorities throughout the hemisphere from an official standpoint looked upon interracial sexual relations with disdain. Religious entities (those based in various sects of Christianity of the time) were disturbed at the mingling of the races. The doctrine of racial separation was crucial to the role of conquest of the hemisphere, and the justification of divine will gave priority to this train of thought which, in turn led to all sorts of actions. Yet the fact of the matter was that women, and especially women of color were the focus of a range of sexual situations from consensual to coercion. Those who found themselves within the confines of white settlements would be caught up in a wide array of often contradictory modes of judgement. Native and black women were giving birth to children of mixed European ancestry in these locales. A different dynamic was occurring in native communities where the situations were more of a consensual nature as men not native to these communities interacted within these settlements because of a variety of circumstances. Regardless of these situations, the disposition and mindset of those in control and seeking to exploit, used the phenomenon of racial mixing to their advantage wherever it was possible. This would often mean entire groups of people no longer existed when it was politically advantageous. In the case of red-black interaction, this meant a community could no longer be "Indian" if there was any amount of African blood present among its population. Thus, if it meant coming out ahead of a situation, the restructuring of a group to conform to white social expectation was an essential component in subjection and, in some instances, the extinction of entire communities of people, at least on paper. The United States Government found it convenient to "terminate" nations of people when it fit into the political scheme of things. Inevitably, these myths are taken as gospel by the general public, and over time (with the help of stereotyping and the dissemination of false information from any number of sources), the myth in the minds of some becomes reality, no matter if it wasn't (isn't) true to begin with. The power of stereotyping must not be underestimated, and image degradation certainly over the centuries has been the rule rather than the exception. This is still a fact today. Tuning into any media venue, especially television and movies, stands in testament to this ongoing situation. One example that has been be stated even in this era, is the perception that, there are no "Indians" left east of the Mississippi River. And as absurd as this sounds, there are still many (and across a wide, cultural spectrum at that) who believe this myth. Despite the efforts by many in Native America who have undertaken and continue to disseminate information via educational endeavors, large segments of mainstream society still hold fast to what an "Indian" should look like and act (for that matter Black, Asian, Hispanic, etc. may be substituted for Indian), whenever and whatever the occasion calls for by the interest of the mainstream. While there are individuals that have contributed to mainstream culture in every facet (government, private industry, social services etc.), some native people who have been involved in educational endeavors continue to be confronted with those who are surprised that native peoples no longer wear buckskins every day, live in tepees or wigwams, and/or actually drive automobiles. While there may be some truth as to what a popular image represents and manifests, it usually does not represent the entire spectrum of experiences and conditions. When examining social phenomenon, the concept of what is monolithic can be deceiving. For anyone or anything that falls outside of that popular perception or perceptions, that situation couldn't possibly be valid, regardless of what the truth of the matter is. The ability to play on stereotypes and misperceptions continues to be used as a tool against communities of color in general. And when this is exploited for whatever gain, the results can be devastating. Whether it be (on whatever level) the efforts of government agencies or the various venues of mainstream media, the re-enforcing of these stereotypes happens on a regular basis, and feeds fuel to the fire that aids in the detrimental effects felt by people of color as a whole. On the state government level, similar acts of legislation served to have a devastating effect that at once denied sovereignty to native nations, and at the same time (on a more subliminal level) fueled the fire of divide and conquer tactics that drove another wedge between native peoples and people of African descent. During 1836 the state of North Carolina enacted legislation that deemed native people as "Free People of Color". The Lumbee people of North Carolina were among those native people to fall victim to the color laws. Struggling to be recognized as native peoples, they were classified at the time as Free People of Color. This directly undermined their efforts in maintaining sovereignty. Being characterized as such, they had no sovereign rights worthy of being respected by those in power. This atmosphere would also set the stage for the Trail of Tears between 1838 and 1839 suffered by the Cherokees. From a legislative perspective, the passage of the Indian Removal Act of 1830, set in motion by Andrew Jackson, fanned the flames that increasingly sought to engulf many Native American communities in the eastern United States. While they were more numerous than some of the other native peoples of North Carolina, Cherokees would face forced removal in spite of the Supreme Court ruling that gave them the legal right to remain in their already shrunken homelands of the Carolinas and Georgia. The administration of President Andrew Jackson contemptuously ignored a Supreme Court ruling issued by Justice John Marshall that allowed Cherokees to stay on their remaining homelands. Blatantly, Jackson ordered the Army to round up Cherokees from their communities in the southeast. Those captured were first placed in concentration camps. Those who eluded the Army would go into hiding, deep in the mountains and forests. In the process of North Carolina enacting their legislation, the gates were open so the state government was able to exploit the situation to their advantage, while further enhancing detrimental effects on both the Native American Communities as well as African-Americans. In the minds of those surviving native people, it was detrimental to acknowledge any influence that was of African origin. This meant, in some instances turning one's back on family. The act of making anything black (on the legislative level) and equating the condition with negativity set the stage (once again) for the type of mental disposition that would steadfastly deny there was no African influence present in any way, shape, or form regardless if it meant common sense was ignored. For to positively acknowledge this was to bring down trouble in any number of incarnations. And given the dire set of circumstances under which many communities were (are) suffering, the thought of consequences that could be implemented by whatever government entity was too much to bear. 1924 would see the Commonwealth of Virginia, with the aid of white supremacsts working for the state's Bureau of Vital Statistics, set into motion events that would lead to the establishing of the Racial Integrity Act, which basically stated (in the eyes of the state) that there were only two races of people in Virginia, white and colored. Yet this type of legislative assault was nothing new. Virginia, as so many other areas of what is now the United States had a long track record that illustrated time and time again the lengths the status quo would go to in order to sway things to their advantage. Dating back to the early 1600s, the courts and legislative bodies of Virginia undertook acts that were to continually erode and deprive the rights of people of African descent, with the native population suffering similar fates. Indeed, the term "colored, was originally deemed to mean anyone with any amount of African blood. This included those of mixed indigenous and European bloodlines. During these early years of European colonization, not all Africans were slaves. The status of "Free People of Color" however, and those who had been manumitted from slavery at best was precarious. There were those who had fallen victim to this horror of enslavement. Some native people(s) had also fallen victim to this fate. One can examine the period of the turn of the 1700s in what is now called South Carolina to find that those who had suffered this horrific fate numerically were native peoples. This certainly would shift numerically as the Trans-Atlantic Slave Trade expanded. There were some whites who were indentured servants. If there was a comparison to be made, the indentured servants had a certain degree of legal protection, minimal as they may have been. An indentured servant did have the possibility of rising out of his situation (white men specifically) and working his way into another social bracket once the period of servitude was concluded. If an indentured servant managed to escape from his or her immediate locale, and especially relocate to an area deemed "frontier", this person stood a chance of avoiding capture because of the ability to blend in with the local white population. Gender as well as racial disparities were the rule, not the exception. Africans, free or enslaved, along with native peoples didn't have much if any chance of improving their lot. As the 1700s progressed, slave and "negro" became to be equated as the same. And where the indentured servant could look eventually to finishing out the length of service, acts of the courts and legislature insured, except for extraordinary circumstances, that those born into or captured and forced into slavery would remain that way for life. A 1691 law stated that the former master of a freed slave was legally obligated to provide transportation of the freed slave(s) out of Virginia within six months. A statute passed in 1705 stated that runaway slaves and those suspected of being a runaway could be dismembered by any white person with the full approval of the law. And while a law passed in 1782 did allow for the freeing of slaves, given the barriers that were in place based on racism, the hopes of empowering one's position presented a formidable obstacle. Some of the legislative acts specifically targeted not only blacks, but those of native descent. The Colonial Legislature did pass a statute in 1657 stating that "Indian children" who had been enslaved were to be set free at the age of 25. No doubt, the colonizing authorities were dictating who was "Indian" and who was not. Many native children would continued to be taken from their families and "Christianized", which meant to be instructed in the ways of civilization. At the time, this approach specifically carried Eurocentric values.

These acts of legislation served to have the state government wreak havoc on the rights of the region's native inhabitants which, in many instances, allocation of resources by government entities were inadequate to begin with. With these actions as precedents, it was not surprising, regardless of how repulsive, that the Racial Integrity Act of 1924 came into being. It was another chapter in a volume of activities that existed since the colonization of that region in a prior century. In the case of Virginia, it would be 1975 before this act was to be repealed. The Civil Rights Movement of the 1950's and 60's was partially responsible for setting the tide in motion that led to the repeal of such acts. Similar legislation compounding racial stratification was enacted after statehood was granted to Oklahoma in 1907. This played into the scenario, which further undermined the rights of anyone of native ancestry, and had a role in the allocation of lands (overseen by the Dawes Commission) that occurred in the wake of the desolvement of national sovereignty. These are only two examples, yet they are hardly unique. There was a period of time when termination fever (during the twentieth century) seemed to be the trend in the legislative chambers on the federal level. At various points in time, the word "termination" may not have been the fashionable phrase of the era, yet the intent was the same, that being to undermine sovereignty and all that it implies. During the 1920s there had (again) been efforts to infringe on indigenous communities on the legislative level. It seems that in spite of the fact that native cultures had governed themselves for centuries, utilizing methods of administration that ranged from simplistic to sophisticated, and had successfully built any number of communities and infrastructures that sustained life and dealt with issues on many levels, government officials, along with other interests once again, determined that indigenous peoples were not capable of making their own decisions. Ironically, in the prior century and the early years of the twentieth century, one premise that had been used against many indigenous people was that they were not citizens of the United States. The twentieth century would bear witness to several legislative efforts that would grant citizenship status to native peoples such as the Indian Citizenship act of 1924 and the Nationality Act of 1940, which actually encompassed the bill of 1924. This was not the first attempt on behalf of the United States to undermine native sovereignty on paper. At the beginning of the year 2000, there were calls again on the legislative level to implement termination. A resolution passed by delegates at the Washington (state) GOP Convention called for an end to tribal governments on reservations in the state. One convention participant was quoted as saying that the military should be used if necessary. As one of several examples, the Treaty of Dancing Rabbit Creek (1830) with the Choctaws of Mississippi in effect made it so that any Choctaw who did not remove to Indian Territory and accept citizenship of the United States was no longer a member of the Choctaw Nation. This type of stipulation was aimed at the other larger nations of the southeast. Basically, the Indian Removal Act placed these communities in the position of being relocated to Indian Territory, or if remaining behind to cease being identified as "Indian". There were varying reactions that ranged from compliance, hiding, and armed resistance. Some Cherokees were to find refuge deep in the mountain areas of North Carolina. Smaller groups of people like the various nations in South Carolina also kept a low profile by trying to remain anonymous. The numerous remaining factions of the Creek Confederacy put up armed resistance in 1836. These factions were living on what remained of their historic ranges in Alabama and Georgia. But the encroaching pressure and actions of white settlements were all too real. Some Creeks actually sought refuge among the Cherokees. Many of these people would end up exiled to Indian Territory, where other members of what had been a strong confederation at one time had preceded them as refugees. Some would be exiled with their brothers and sisters who comprised the Confederacy. Others would suffer with the Cherokees when their time of horror arrived. Seminole resistance would prove to be the most persistent, although many of their numbers who had not been killed or enslaved would also find themselves bound for Indian Territory.

Yet as many people knew and were aware, the promise of social equality on paper and the reality of life are not one in the same. As with other groups of people of non-white backgrounds living in the United States, discrimination and injustice were companions that were more the rule as opposed to the exception.

The provisions of the Fourteenth Amendment (Equal Protection Clause) has a way of being ignored when circumstances deem it sociopolitically convenient. There has also been a long history of state and federal government agencies ignoring rights that are legally protected when it is advantageous to do so. If in fact this process was successful, the domino effect would be that no government entity on the federal, state or local level would bear any responsibility(ies) to the now terminated nation.

This began to gather steam in Congress during 1946. There was a feeling that this would undermine and destabilize traditional values, thus setting the climate for the end of tribal government and cultural identity. Whatever land base that in the majority of cases, was already a fraction of what was historically evident, would again be in jeopardy from any number of outside entities. By 1953, formal legislation in Congress was well underway with the implementation of House Concurrent Resolution 108 and Public Law 280. Yet damage had already been in the process of happening as sovereign communities fell under attack. The Menominee of Wisconsin as one example suffered this indignity beginning in 1947, when the federal government began to apply administrative pressures which, after a struggle (that exceeded fourteen years) lost their status as a sovereign nation (the actual termination occurring in 1961. The Menominee were not able to restore their government-to-government relationship on a federal level again until 1974. Many nations of people of Long Island (New York) such as the Unkechaug, the Montauk, different bands of Wampanoag in New England such as the Mashpee of Cape Cod, the Lumbee of North Carolina, the Ramapough of northern New Jersey-south New York, the Mowa Choctaw of Alabama, the Yuchis in Oklahoma, and the Chinooks of Washington, are only some of the groups of people having to deal with this indignity perpetrated on their respective community identities from the various government agencies (on the federal level) that refuse to recognize them as a sovereign people. While there had been initial shock at what was happening, people in urban areas, as well as on reservations, began to organize to deal with the situations that had sent waves of uncertainty into their midst. The National Congress of American Indians, which was formed in 1944, as well as other groups and coalitions across the United States came together to stem the tide of termination. Another such organization is the United Southern and Eastern Tribes, a coalition of eastern nations (that have federal recognition status), was formed in 1968. This organization was originally known as the United Southeastern Tribes. At the time of its formation, this coalition was comprised of the Miccosukees, the Seminole Tribe of Florida, The Mississippi Band of Choctaws, and the Eastern Band of Cherokees. By the beginning of the twenty- first century, it was to comprise of most of the federally recognized nations of the eastern United States. Other organizations would form throughout the United States in the latter part of the twentieth century, often having in their respective constituencies people of native descent who were not necessarily enrolled with any recognized nation. As the year 2000 progressed, there was a perception in the minds of some that the census undertaken by the United States Government was another possible attempt to legislate people and communities to paper oblivion. In what is now the United States, and arguably throughout the western hemisphere, national identities have been forged, and these identities have been implemented for the most part by the conquerors of whatever region is examined predominately Anglo in North America, Spanish in the Caribbean, Central and South America, with French, Dutch, and Portuguese also having influences). What has supposedly been locked into place (from an administrative and/or bureaucratic standpoint) are the categories of racial identification, at least as far as government interests are concerned. The identification of peoples into narrow definitions of categories was born out of the need to exploit those who were to be victimized. These characterizations often distort the reality because of the need to maintain ideologies that keep existing sociopolitical structures in place. What is frightening is that it appears that many victims, as well as victimizers, have fallen for the stereotypes, and all play a hand for whatever reason in maintaining these images, no matter what the consequences. The Council of the Seminole Nation of Oklahoma in a referendum of July 1, 2000, set the stage for the removal from their nation by proposing a blood quantum of one eighth. While a spokesperson for the nation indicated there was a concern as far as seeing the bloodline thin out, unfortunately, factors play into this scenario that have more telling consequences. Those of African descent classified as "Freedman" found themselves in circumstances that could draw parallels to the turbulent period before, during, and immediately after the Civil War of 1861 through 65. This was happening in an atmosphere that had seen the Freedman Bands (Caesar Brunner and Dosar Barkus) struggle on a legal level with factions within the council over rights issues. It was during the mid 1990s when the Freedman Bands enlisted the assistance of the NAACP Legal Defense Fund to aid in their struggle. While the proposition (Proposed Amendment 7) voted on during the summer of 2000 did not qualify as a mandate due to the numbers of representatives who voted against it (423 for and 292 against), it set an ominous tone. The Bureau of Indian Affairs was supposed to have the final say. In October of 2001, the Bureau of Indian Affairs (BIA) intervened in this matter by refusing to recognize tribal actions, and by taking away the Seminole Nation of Oklahoma's right to administer federal monies. The BIA, as well as other agencies, would also refuse to recognize an elected administration, who came into office in August of 2001. This was headed by Chief Ken Chambers, who unseated former chief, Jerry Haney. This would lead to the accusation of unfair dealings from the BIA (something not new) by leaders from the Seminole Nation of Oklahoma (S.N.O.). With the passage of a resolution set forth by the council of the S.N.O. reinstating the Freedmen, the Bureau of Indian Affairs lifted its restrictions on federal monies that had been withheld. Yet even though they had been technically reinstated, the Freedmen were still not eligible for all of the benefits other members of the S.N.O. enjoyed. By the fall of 2002, this issue was still proving to be divisive, as some factions backed Jerry Haney as chief, who was recognized as the legitimate leader of the Seminole Nation of Oklahoma, by the Bureau of Indian Affairs. On the other hand, there was a faction backing Ken Chambers as Chief. He had been elected by members of the Seminole Nation of

Oklahoma. But as the electorate had excluded black members from voting, the Bureau of Indian Affairs refused to recognize Chambers as a leader. Fistfights were being reported as happening between the two factions. In late 2003, this issue was still unresolved.

Although related, The Seminole Nation of Oklahoma and the Seminole Tribe of Florida are two autonomous entities. Articles that appeared in spring issues of the Seminole Tribune, published by the Seminole Tribe of Florida, articulated how the matter of blood quantum has affected those living on the reservations in Florida. Yet there was still a sense of community among other Seminole People, and the willingness to reach out to those of shared ancestry.

In April of 2001, tribal Chairman James Billie of the Seminole Tribe of Florida (at that time) made an unannounced visit to the small community of Red Bays on the northern tip of Andros Island in the Bahamas. It was here that the chairman made contact with descendants of Seminoles who escaped from Florida during the Second Seminole War. It is believed that the first of the migrations started around 1838 and was to continue over a twenty-year period. This is another branch of the Seminole diaspora (in terms of communities). There still exists communities in Texas and Mexico. This does not include those of Seminole descent outside of these communities that proudly recognize and acknowledge a shared heritage.

As this dynamic was playing itself into numerous scenarios across the United States, the time honored phenomenon of living continues. As during the time "Indian Territory" was in a state of (semi) autonomy, there were and are people who concern themselves with the course of living, regardless of whatever political power plays were occurring. People continued to interact with friends and family regardless of whatever government entity or those who tried to endear themselves to those entities did (or do). While maintaining a cultural base, many continued life with those of the same perspective and, in some instances, this meant (means) those who are identifiable as part of community looked at a panorama of skin colors and hairtypes. The issue of blood quantum was (is) seen by some in reservation communities as another way to further divide the people. In the Traditionalist mindset, there is only the issue of who is of the people, and bloodlines are not necessarily the ruling factor. Not that there had not been issues of multiple ancestry addressed in various communities. Some members of a respective community realized there was (is) a larger picture that needed serious consideration. While some in political power spout rhetoric, espousing brotherhood and the breaking down of barriers, other sources across a number of spectrums continue on the march to further undermine the sovereignty of reservation communities and the manipulation of who is eligible for tribal membership. The fact that those perpetuating these ideals live in a respective community and may have skin contents that contain melanin to whatever degree plays into the time tried and tested tactic(s) of divide and conquer. Similarly, in urban scenarios, people of native descent experience similar sets of circumstances as far as the issue of blood quantum is concerned. There were (are) those who approve of the thought of meeting this criteria, as well as those who see it as divisive. Many of this particular train of logic see the danger that in the eyes of government, this was (is) another step on the road to extinction, at least on paper. And while this possibility exists, there are those who will certainly continue to maintain strong cultural perspectives and retention no matter what happens. Through supposed termination (in the bureaucratic sense), warfare, disease, and slavery, men and women did what they could to hold on to and pass down legacies as best as they could under horrific circumstances that seemed to continue to mushroom into a variety of forms. This has certainly been the case since October 12, 1492. The danger is there may no longer be "tribes" or "nations" as is commonly thought. This would mean whatever resources had been protected by a sovereign entity would no longer be a fact as outsiders, be they government or big businesses erode and engulf what they can take away. In this scenario, there are no more "Indians" left. This situation certainly has centuries of precedents.

ACKNOWLEDGEMENTS

While I have been conducting research since 1972, I actually began work on this project in 1994. As is life, there have been many trails and tribulations. On the positive side, there have been many people and some institutions that deserve higher accolades than I can bestow. I certainly hope to include everyone, so I'm giving this my best shot.

In terms of libraries, there is the Huntington Free Library of the Bronx, New York, which for a time housed the greatest collection of books and documents on the indigenous peoples of this hemisphere. This is a resource that is sorely missed today. The Dorothy Scott Osceola Library on the Hollywood Seminole Indian Reservation, Hollywood Florida, that was gracious enough to allow me to use it as a resource in the Summer of 1995, and the Schomburg Center for Research on Black Culture of Harlem, New York.

As for as individuals: Giselle May (there are truly no words I could ever say that could express my gratitude). Devorah Hill, Francesca Burgess, along with Dr.Heriberto Dixon (who has shared many of his findings with me over the years), all of whom turned me on to Jack Forbes within forty eight hours of conversations held individually during the early 1990s. Govinda Sanyal, who I have shared hours of insightful conversations for more than a decade (the phone companies rejoice). Kevin Thompson and Tracy Cook, for their feedback on the manuscript draft. My mother, Gladys Harrington, who took me on visits to what was then the Dania Seminole Indian Reservation (now Hollywood) when I was a child. Two of my all time favorite Pow Wow Trail buddies, this being my son Harlon, and daughter Nzingha. Bethanna Ferguson, mother of the Torn Pages Project, and a lady whose heart is bigger than the Everglades. "Doc" John Hotvedt, who has put up with the technologically challenged for decades. Ramon Nunez, an educator in the public school system of New York City, who let me borrow a book from his desk (I promise I'll return it). Gwen Craig for helping me with an administrative matter. The numerous individuals who graciously shared their family stories with me. And last but certainly not least, the brothers and sisters that made up the many incarnations of the Drum Circle Singers.

BIBLIOGRAPHY

Abel, Annie Heloise - The American Indian as Slaveholder and Seccessionist, University of Nebraska Press, Lincoln, Nebraska, and London, England, 1992

Baker, T. and Julia P. eds - The WPA Oklahoma Slave Narratives - University of Oklahoma Press, Norman, Oklahoma, and London, England, 1996

Ballantine, Betty and Ian eds - The Native Americans, An Illustrated History, Turner Publishing, Atlanta, Georgia, 1993

Bennett, Lerone Jr.- The Shaping of Black America: The Struggles and Triumphs of African Americans 1619 to the 1990's, Penquin Books, New York, New York, 1975

Bird, Traveller - Tell Them They Lie, The Sequoyah Myth, Western Lore Publisher, Los Angeles, California, 1971

Bolster, W. Jeffrey, Black Jacks: African American Seamen in the Age of Sail - Harvard University Press, Cambridge, Massachusettes, September 1998

Brooks, Lester - Great Civilizations of Ancient Africa, Four Winds Press, New York, New York, 1971

Buckland, John Alexander - The Wiechquaeskeck Indians of Southwestern Connecticut in the Seventeenth Century, Heritage Books, Bowie, Maryland, 2002

Burt, Jesse and Ferguson, Robert B.- Indians of the Southeast Then and Now, Abingdon Press, Nashville Tenn, and New York N.Y. 1973

Burton, Arthur- Black, Buckskins, and Blue: African American Scouts and Soldiers on the Frontier, Eakin Press, Austin, Texas, 1999

Burton, Arthur - Black, Red, and Deadly: Black and Indian Gunfighters of the Indian Territory, 1870-1907, Eakin Press, 1991

Byrd, William L. and Smith John H. - North Carolina Slaves and Free People of Color, Hyde and Beaufort Counties, Heritage Books, Bowie, Maryland, 2002

Calloway, Colin G. - The American Revolution in Indian Country: Crises and Diversity in Native American Communities, Cambridge University Press, Cambridge, England, 1995

Carew, Jan - Fulcrums of Change: Origins of Racism in the Americas and Other Essays, Africa World Press, April 1988

Carroll, John editor - The Black Military Experience In The American West,

Liveright Publishing, New York, New York 1973

Churchill, Ward, and Wall, James Vander - <u>Agents of Repression: The FBI's Secret War Against the Black Panther Party and the American Indian Movement,</u> South End Press, Boston, Massachsettes, 1998

Downs, Dorothy - <u>The Art of the Florida Seminole and Miccosukee Indians,</u> University Press of Florida, Gainesville, Florida, 1995

Durham, Philip and Jones, Everett L.- <u>The Negro Cowboys,</u> Bison Books, University of Nebraska Press, Lincoln Nebraska, and London England, 1983

Edgerton, Robert B. - <u>Like Lions They Fought: The Zulu War and the Last Black Empire in South Africa,</u> Ballantine Books, New York, New York, 1988

Edmunds, David R. editor - <u>American Indian Leaders,</u> University of Nebraska Press, Lincoln, Nebraska, and London, England, 1980

Fell, Barry - <u>America B.C.,</u> Pocket Books, New York, New York, 1976

Fixico, Donald L. - <u>The Urban Indian Experience In America,</u> University of New Mexico Press, Albuquerque, New Mexico, 2000

Forbes, Jack - <u>Africans and Native Americans: The Language of Race and the Evolution of Red-Black Peoples,</u> University of Illinois Press, Urbana, and Chicago, Illinois, 1993

Foreman, Grant - <u>The Five Civilized Tribes,</u> University of Oklahoma Press, Norman, Oklahoma 1934

Gaillard, Frye and Demeritt, Caroline - <u>As Long As the Waters Flow: Native Americans in the South and East,</u> - John F. Blair, Publisher, Winston-Salem, North Carolina, 1998

Gonzalez, Juan - <u>Harvest of Empire: A History of Latin America,</u> Penquin Books, New York, New York, 2000

Green, Michael - <u>The Politics of Indian Removal,</u> University of Nebraska Press, Lincoln, Nebraska, and London, England, 1982

Grumet, Robert editor - <u>Northeastern Indian Lives 1632 - 1816,</u> University of Massachusetts Press, Amherst, Massachusettes, 1996

Guillemin, Jeanne - <u>Urban Renegades: The Cultural Strategy of American Indians,</u> Columbia University Press, New York, New York, and London, England, 1975

Guinn, Jeff - <u>Our Land Before We Die,</u> Jeremy P. Tarcher/Putnam, New York, New York, 2002

Hall, Gwendolyn Midlo - <u>Africans in Colonial Louisisana: The Development of Afro-Creole Culture in the Eigteenth Century,</u> Louisiana State University Press, Baton Rouge, Louisiana, and London England, 1995

Harris, Joseph - <u>Africans and Their History</u> - Mentor Books, New York, New York and Ontario, Canada, 1987

Hauptman, Laurence - <u>Between Two Fires: American Indians in the Civil War, Free Press Paperbacks,</u> New York, New York, 1996

Hauptman, Laurence H. - <u>Tribes and Tribulations: Misconceptions about American Indians and their Histories,</u> University of New Mexico Press, Albuququerque, New Mexico, 1995

Hemming, John - <u>Red Gold - The Conquest of the Brazilian Indians 1500 -</u>

1760 Harvard University Press, Cambridge, Massachusettes, 1978

Higginbotham, A. Leon Jr. - In The Matter of Color Race and The American Legal Process: The Colonial Period, Oxford Paperbacks, Oxford, England, New York, New York, Toronto, Canada, and Melbourne, Australia, 1981

Hudson, Charles - The Southeastern Indians, University of Tenessee Press, Knoxville, Tennessee, 1976

Irwin, Graham W. - Africans Abroad, Columbia University Press, New York, New York, 1977

Jahoda, Gloria - The Trail of Tears, Wings Books, New York, New York, and Avenel, New Jersey, 1995

James, C.L.R. - The Black Jacobins: Toussaint L'Overture and the San Domingo Revolution - C.L.R. James, Vintage Books, New York New York 1989

Josephy, Alvin Jr. editor - America in 1492: The World of Indian People Before the Arrival of Columbus, Vantage Books, New York, N.Y., 1993

Josphey, Alvin Jr. - The Patriot Chiefs, Penquin Books, New York, New York, 1976

Katz, William Loren , Black Legacy: A History of New York's African Americans, Antheneum Books, New York, New York, 1997

Katz, William Loren - The Black West, Doubleday Anchor Books, Garden City New York, 1973

Kerns, Virginia - Women and the Ancestors, Black Carib Kinship and Ritual, University of Illinois Press, Urbana and Chicago, Illinois, October 1997

Kilson, Martin and Rotberg, Robert, eds - The African Diaspora, Harvard University Press, Cambridge, Massachusettes, and London, England, 1976

Kniffen, Fred B., Gregory, Hiram F., and Stokes, George A. - The Historic Tribes of Louisiana From 1542 to the Present, Louisiana State University Press, Baton Rouge, Louisiana, and London, England, 1987

LaDuke, Winona - All Our Relations: Native Struggles for Land and Life, South End Press Cambridge Massachusettes, 1999

LaVere, David - Contrary Neighbors: Southern Plains and Removed Indians in Indian Territory, University of Oklahoma Press, Norman, Oklahoma, 2000

Littlefield, Daniel - Africans and Creeks: From the Colonial Period to the Civil War, Greenwood Press, Westport, Connecticut, and London, England, 1979

Littlefield, Daniel F. Jr. - The Chickasaw Freedmen: A People Without A Country, Greenwood Press, Westport, Connecticut, and London, England, 1980

Linsey, Donal F. Jr., - Indians at Hampton Institute 1877-1923, University of Illinios Press, Urbana, Illinois 1995

May, Katja - African Americans and Native Americans in the Creek and Cherokee Nations, 1830 - 1920, Garland Publishing, New York, New York, and London, England, 1996

Matthiessen, Peter - Indian Country, Penquin Books, New York, N.Y. 1992

McReynolds, Edwin C. - The Seminoles, University of Oklahoma Press, Norman, Oklahoma, 1957

Meltzer, Milton - Slavery: A World History, De Capo Press, New York New York, 1993

Mulroy. Kevin - <u>Freedom on the Border: The Seminole Maroons in Florida,</u> <u>the Indian Territory, Coahuila, and Texas,</u> Texas Tech University Press, Lubbock Texas, 1993

Plane, Anne Marie - <u>Colonial Intimacies: Indian Marriage in Colonial New</u> <u>England,</u> Cornell University Press, Ithaca, New York, and London, England, 2000

Paredes, J.Anthony editor - <u>Indians of the Southeastern United States in the</u> <u>Late 20th Century,</u> University of Alabama Press, Tuscaloosa, Alabama, and London, England, 1992

Pasay, Marcella Houle - <u>Full Circle: A Directory of Native and African</u> <u>Americans in Windham County Connecticut, and Vicinity, 1650- 1900 Volumes</u> <u>1 and 2</u> Heritage Books, Bowie, Maryland, 2002

Perdue, Theda - <u>Nations Remembered: The Oral History of the Cherokees,</u> <u>Chickasaws, Choctaws, Creeks, and Seminoles in Oklahoma 1865-1907,</u> University of Oklahoma Press, Norman, Oklahoma, and London, England, 1993

Perdue, Theda - <u>Slavery and the Evolution of Cherokee Society, 1540- 1866,</u> University of Tennessee Press, Knoxville, Tennessee, 1979

Price, Richard editor - <u>Maroon Societies: Rebel Slave Communities in the</u> <u>Americas,</u> John Hopkins University Press, Baltimore, Maryland, and London, England, 1979

Pritchard, Evan T. - <u>Native New Yorkers: The Legacy of the Algonquin</u> <u>People of New York,</u> Council Oaks Books, Tulsa Oklahoma, 2002

Prucha, Francis Paul editor - <u>Documents of American Indian Policy,</u> University of Nebraska Press, Lincoln, Nebraska, and London, England, 1975

Read, William A. - <u>Florida Place Names of Indian Origin and Seminole</u> <u>Personal Names,</u> Fire Ant Books, University of Alabama Press, Tuscaloosa, Alabama, 2004

Reese Ted - <u>Soft Gold: A History of the Fur Trade in the Great Lakes Region</u> <u>and its impact on Native American Culture,</u> Heritage Books, Bowie, Maryland, 2001

Rights, Douglas L. - <u>The American Indian in North Carolina,</u> John F. Blair, Publisher, Winston-Salem, - North Carolina, 1957

Russell Howard S. - <u>Indian New England Before The Mayflower,</u> University Press of New England, Hanover, New Hampshire, and London England, 1980

Ruttenber, E.M. - <u>Indian Tribes of Hudson's River Volumes 1 and 2,</u> Hope Farm Press, Saugerties New York, 1992

Sanders, Ronald - <u>Lost Tribes and Promised Lands: The Origin of American</u> <u>Racism,</u> HarperPerrenial Books, New York N.Y., 1992

Simmons, William - <u>Notices of East Florida,</u> University of Florida Press, Bicentennial Floridiana Facsimile Series, Gainesville, Florida 1973

Strong, John - <u>We Are Still Here, The Algonquian Peoples of Long Island</u> <u>Today,</u> Empire State Books, Interlaken, New York, 1998

Strong, John A. - <u>The Algonquian Peoples of Long Island from Earliest</u> <u>Times to 1700,</u> Empire State Books, Interlaken, New York, 1997

Trelease, Alan W.- <u>Indian Affairs in Colonial New York: The Seventeenth</u>

Century, Bison Books, Lincoln, Nebraska, and London, England, 1997

Usner H. Daniel - Indians, Settlers, and Slaves in a Frontier Exchange Economy: The Lower Mississippi Valley Before 1783, University of North Carolina Press, Chapel Hill, North Carolina, 1992

Van Sertimer, Ivan - Early America Revisited, Transaction Publishers, New Brunswick, New Jersey, and London, England, 1998

Van Sertimer, Ivan editor - The African Presence in Early America, Transaction Publishers, New Brunswick, New Jersey, and London, England, 1992

Van Sertimer, Ivan - They Came Before Columbus, Random House, New York, New York, 1976

Waldman, Carl - Encyclopedia of Native American Tribes, Facts on File, China, 1988

Wallace, Anthony F.C. - The Long Bitter Trail: Andrew Jackson and the Indians, Hill and Wang, New York, New York, 1993

Weyler, Rex - Blood of the Land: The Government and Corporate War Against First Nations, New Society Publishers, Philadelphia, Pennsylvania, and Gabriola Island, B.C., Canada, 1992

Weatherford, Jack - Indian Givers, Ballantine Books, New York New York, 1990

Weatherford, Jack - Native Roots: How The Indians Enriched America, Columbine - Ballantine Books, New York, New York, 1991

Weatherford, Jack - Savages and Civilization; Who Will Survive? Columbine - Ballantine Books, New York, New York, 1994

Wickham, Patricia - Osceola's Legacy, University of Alabama Press, Tuscaloosa, Alabama, and London, England, 1991

Williams, Walter L. - Southeastern Indians Since the Removal Era, University of Georgia Press, Athens, Ga. 1979

Wood, Peter H. - Black Majority: Negroes in Colonial South Carolina from 1670 Through The Stono Rebellion, W.W. Norton and Company, New York, New York, London England, 1975

Wood, Peter, Waselkov, Gregory L., Hatley, M. Thomas eds. - Powhatan's Mantle: Indians in the Colonial Southeast, University of Nebraska Press, Lincoln, Nebraska, and London England, 1989

Wright, J. Leitch Jr.- Creeks and Seminoles, University of Nebraska Press, Lincoln, Nebraska, and London, England, 1986

Wright, J. Leitch Jr. - The Only Land They Knew: The Tragic Story of the American Indians in the Old South, The Free Press New York, New York, 1971

Internet/Website Sources

"Red, Black, and White in the Old South"
http://users.rcn.com/wovoka/Pmchap1.htm
"The Crucible of American Indian Identity: Native Tradition versus Colonial Imposition in Postconquest North America" - Ward Churchill, http:www.zmag.org/ZMag/articles/jan98ward.htm

Publication/Periodical Sources

Belue, Ted Franklin -"Did Daniel Bone Kill Pompey the Black Shawnee at the 1778 Seige of Boonesborough", Filson Club History Quarterly - January 1993 vol 67, #1 P.5-22

Florida Humanities Council Forum - Fall 1992 vol. XVI #2, "Florida's Native Americans"

Latino Village Press - October 16- November 15,1994, "The Taino Warrior" ,by Bobby Gonzalez

News From Indian Country: Late August 2001 - "Establish blood quantum for benefits"

Mid October 2001, "Answers hidden in lost Black Seminole village, Scott McCabe

Late August 2002 - "Mohawk Ironworkers build New York: Booming Out"

Mid October 2002 - "Judge rules in Seminole Nation leadership dispute"

Late October 2002, "Seminole circulate petition to oust Haney"

Newcomb, Steven T.- The Native American Struggle: Conquering the Rule of Law A Colloquim, The Evidence of Chrisitian Nationalism in Federal Indian Law: The Doctrine of Discovery, Johnson vs. McIntosh, and Plenary Power, New York University Review of Law and Social Change, P. 303-341

Wild West - February 2000 - "Buffalo Soldiers in Utah Territory" by Robert Forster, and "Chief Colorow, Symbol of Ute Resistance, Never Wanted to Give Up His Colorado Home", by Richard M.Simmons

June 2001 - "Killer of Pain's Transcontinental Jouney", by Dale L. Walker

INDEX

Appalachicola 18,41
Appalachicola River 44
Arapaho 10,54,82,84
Apartheid 3,104
Arawak 7,14
Arbuckle, Matthew 64,66
Arizona 83,85,105
Arkansas 19,46,63,64,73,74,83
Asia 15,27,60
Asians 10,97,103,104,109
Atomic Bomb 105
Attakullakulla 62
Attucks, Crispus 39
Aymara 6
Bahamas 8,14,115
Bambara 29,97,102
Bannock 54
Barbados 17
Barkus, Dosar 79,114
Battle of Bear Valley 83
Battle of Bowlegs Town 45
Battle of Chustenahlah 74,75
Battle of Greasy Grass (Little Bighorn) 53,88
Battle of Honey Springs 76,77
Battle of Horseshoe Bend 44
Battle of Round Mountain 74
Bay River 31
Beam Family 69,70
Belgian Congo 10
Belgium 11
Belize 4
Berlin Conference of 1884-5 12
Big Cypress Swamp 46
Billie, James 115
Bird Creek 74
Black Hills 106
Black Kettle 10,86
Black Fish 27
Blackfoot 53,54,85
Black Panther Party 106,107
Blood Quantum 2,3,89,102,108,114,115
Bonga, George 100,101
Bonga, Pierre 100
Boone, Daniel 27
Boonesborough 27

Jackson, Andrew 43-6,72,110
Jaguaripe 28
Jamaica 56
Jefferson, Thomas 17
Jim Crow Laws 104
Johnson, Grant 80
Kansas 64,73-76,81
Kaws 88
Kawita 48
Kenhadjo 45
Kentucky 27,36,63
Kenya 10
Keyawee 34
Kieft, William 22,23
King George War 41
Kickapoo 67,68
Kiowa 54,85
Kituwahs 62
Kootenay 54
Ku Klux Klan 49
Kuwait 50
Lagunna De Parras 86
Lake Miccosukee 45,59
Lakota 53,54,62,82-84,87,105,106
Lakota Sioux Dance Theater 107
Lane, James 74
Lanre, George 80
La Venta 7
Lawson, John 31
Lee, Robert E. 78
Lenape 35,61,98
Lewis and Clark 55,82
Libya 50
Lighthorse 65,68,80
Long Island 22,23,35,113
Louisiana 19,36,63,85,97
Louisiana Native Guard 83
Love, Nat 49
Loverture, Toussaint 39
Lowry, Henry Berry 48,49
Lucayo 8,14
Lumbee 48,49,109,113
Macaco 29
Macintosh, D.N. 74
Macintosh, James 74,75

MacDonald, Peter 50
Mackenzie, Alexander 82
Macumba 95
Mahican 21,98
Malcom X 52
Mali 6,9
Mandan 54,61
Manhattan 9,21-3,47
Mansa Musa 9
Marianna 47
Maroon 10,15,26,28,29,36-38,47,56,59,85,97
Marshall, John 110
Mashantucket(Pequot) 23,96,105
Mashpee 113
Matamoros 86
Matchapungas 31
Mattaponi 17,59
Matrilineal 26,57
May, Cornelius Jacobsen 22
Mayan 7
McIntosh, D.N. 74
McJunkin, George 107
McKinley, William 90
Mecca 9
Mediterranean Sea 8
Meherrin 31
Melungeon 103
Menominee 113
Meso America 7
Mestizo 30,47
Metacom (King Philip) 20
Metis 3,4
Mexica 7
Mexican Government 68,86
Mexico 7,8,10,29,30,44,49,53,60,63,68,69,85,86,97,115
Mexico City 10,29,60,94
Miccosukees 41,106,113
Michilimackinac 21
Miller, Zeke 80
Minnesota 100,101
Minuit, Peter 22
Mississippi 19,59,61,63,70,96,104,112,113
Mississippi River 9,38,39,55,63,82,94,109
Mississippian 7
Missouri 64,85

Missouri River 9
Mobile 42
Mohawk 21,99,105
Mohawk River 21
Mohegan 23
Mohican 22
Montauk 98,113
Mowa Choctaw 113
Monroe Presidency 46
Montaukett 35
Montreal 21
Moore, Maurice 33
Mountpleasant, Clinton 77
Mulatto 16,17,30,47,48
Muscogee 41,98
Muskogean 10,48,57
Mustee 16,30,47
NAACP Legal Defense Fund 114
Nakota 82
Nacimiento 86
Namibia 11
Nanticoke 98
Narragansett 10,23,98
Natanapalle 36
Natchez 7,36
Natick 39
National Congress of American Indians 113
National Sacrifice Area 105
Nationality Act of 1940 112
Native American 2,14,15,18,19,21,24-30,34-
36,41,48,60,70,73,77,86,93,94,96,97,101-104,107,110
Nave, Charley 76
Nazi Germany 3
Neamathla 45
Necho II 8
Negro Fort 44,45
Neues River 31
New Amsterdam 21-23
New Bern 31,32
New England 10,23,25,113
New Mexico 9,37,85,105,107
New Netherland 22
New Orleans 24,36,38,39,50,85
New York 1,10,19,21,32,35,36,47,54,77,85,105,107,113
New York City 9,19,20,22,23,95,107

Red Bay 115
Redbone 103
Redbone, Martha 107
Red Cloud 83,84
Red Stick 44
Red Sea 8
Reeves, Bass 80,81
Reno Marcus 88
Ridge Faction 71
Riel's Rebellion 1869 and 1889 3
Roatan 4
Rock Island 94
Rocky Mountains 54,82
Rosewood 60
Ross, John 72,73
Rufus Buck Gang 80
Russians 82
Sac and Fox 59,94
Saint Lawrence 21
Saint Marks 45
Saint Augustine 33,42,67
Saint Kitts 56
Saint Louis 62,94
Saint Vincent 4
San Juan Hill 86
San Lorenzo 7
San Lorenzo de los Negros 29
San Miguel De Guadalupe 16
Sand Creek 10,86
Santee 19,87
Santeria 95
Santo Domingo 15
Saponi 34,98
Sara 34
Saudi Arabia 50
Saura 34
Saukenuk 94
Savannah River 25,32
Savannahs 48
Savanukah 62
Saxapahaw 34
Saxapaws 32
Scottish 48,57
Second Indian Home Guard 76,77
Second Kansas Colored 75,76,83